FAITH
AND CULTURE

For Paul & Jody
With hopes of ongoing
conversations about the
meeting of faith & culture.

FAITH AND CULTURE

Musings at the Juncture of Faith and Culture in the 21st Century

COMPILED BY JIM SYMONS

author HOUSE®

AuthorHouse™ LLC
1663 Liberty Drive
Bloomington, IN 47403
www.authorhouse.com
Phone: 1-800-839-8640

Published by AuthorHouse   12/18/2013

ISBN: 978-1-4918-4356-7 (sc)
ISBN: 978-1-4918-4355-0 (e)

Library of Congress Control Number: 2013922761

Contents

Introduction vii
              Jim Symons

Chapter 1   One, But Not The Same 1
              Gary Demarest

Chapter 2   Hispanic Christians In The U.S. Today 17
              Jane Atkins Vasquez

Chapter 3   Life Experiences In The Gospel Of John 32
              F. Dale Bruner

Chapter 4   "Religious" Manifestations In A Modernizing China ...58
              Franklin Woo

Chapter 5   Where Muslims And Christians Meet:
           Political And Missional Issues 87
              Dudley Woodberry

Chapter 6   Korean Unity—Seeking for One Flag in Place
           of the Two: The Christian Pilgrimage in Korea 99
              Joseph Kang

Acknowledgments 125

About the Authors 127

INTRODUCTION

How does faith impact culture?

What influence does culture have on faith?

These questions might seem academic, limited to university religion or philosophy classes, until we look at the morning headlines or listen to the evening newscasts. Our lives are invaded daily by stories of extremists with yet another suicide bombing, or protests for and against reproductive rights or end of life issues, or scientific discoveries raising questions about the creation of the universe—all based on conflicting faith commitments. Like it or not, these faith/culture questions are part of all of our lives.

Discussions of the way faith and culture engage each other are common at Monte Vista Grove (or 'The Grove'), a community of retired Presbyterian ministers and missionaries where I live. While sharing a common Christian denominational background, residents have viewpoints on political, religious and social issues that run the gamut of right to left. Color us not red or blue, but purple. Many of us have spent most of our adult years outside the United States, immersed in countries and cultures around the world, so there is a wide spectrum of experience and opinions on every current issue. Some of us have wondered, "Why keep this rich dialogue to our selves? Maybe we could involve the wider community."

With this in mind, in January, 2012, a series of lectures on the current juncture of faith and culture was launched at The Grove. We chose a title: *Monte Vista MUSINGS*. As Gary Demarest writes in the first chapter, the word *musing* means "absorbed in thought, especially to turn something over in the mind meditatively and often inconclusively." Speakers were chosen who represented different cultural perspectives and life experiences. This book is a compilation of the first six lectures, three in 2012 and three in 2013. Some of the speakers changed or added to their original talks to make their writings more comprehensive and up to date at the time of publication in September, 2013.

The words *faith* and *culture* are dynamic, not static. Over time they take on new meanings. In the Christian tradition, for centuries faith meant the total life of a follower of Jesus. But in the last three centuries of the Enlightenment, many have come to see faith as a rational set of *beliefs* that are often separated from the way a person lives. In the chapters of this book there is an effort to describe faith as a way of life that sometimes supports current dimensions of culture, and sometimes opposes them. Since faith is a personal response to God, there are as many different expressions of faith as there are people. Instead of seeing this as a problem, each of our writers presents the juncture of faith and culture from their personal experience and we are all enriched by the differences.

An alternative understanding is to speak not just of *my* faith but of *the* faith, as in the Muslim or Jewish or Christian faiths. This collective use of the term will be explored in this book as we look at ideology (conservatives and liberals in chapter one), ethnicity (Hispanic Christians in chapter two), national traditions (China and Korea in chapters four and six), interfaith relations (the meeting of Muslims and Christians in chapter five), and historical context (Christian community in Biblical perspective, chapter three). Faith never takes place in a vacuum, but arises within different cultural experiences as this book demonstrates. To understand this process we need to look at the meaning of *culture.*

Sociologist Peter Berger, writing in his book <u>The Sacred Canopy,</u> describes human beings as *world-building creatures.* That is, we must make a world for ourselves to survive, and the world we make is culture. Its purpose is to provide firm structures for human life that are lacking biologically. For example, tools are made to modify our physical environment for survival in a threatening world. Language is produced and permeates every aspect of life. It is human nature to produce a world, including social networks and institutions. What appears at any historical moment as "human nature" is itself a product of our world-building activity.

Berger describes the process of world building in three moments or steps—externalization, objectivation, and internalization. <u>Externalization</u> is the ongoing outpouring of human energy into the world both in physical and mental activity, continuously shaping new cultural possibilities. Only a few of these survive to the next step. <u>Objectivation</u> is the attainment of a reality based on some of these cultural possibilities that confront us humans as something external to us even though we created it. <u>Internalization</u> is the way we take objective reality and make it subjective so that our understanding of reality is altered and human life is transformed.

The American experience of racism can serve as an example. Externalization—for three hundred years, slavery and segregation were based on a choice made by white people that black people were inferior and should be subjugated to the point of being property to be bought and sold. This concept was backed by laws and guns. Objectivation— black people were captured in Africa and transported as property on ships across the ocean to become slaves on American plantations. Internalization—a subjective belief system arose where white people <u>knew</u> they were superior to their slave property, and many black people came to <u>know</u> they were inferior.

The whole process of slavery was cultural, a product of the human capacity for world building. This meant that a new externalization could replace slavery. Berger suggests in <u>The Sacred Canopy</u> that faith could be the source of change. The sacred canopy is the religious endorsement by people of faith that protects or covers a culture, or some part of it. Southern plantation owners found Biblical passages that would <u>prove</u> slavery was ordained by God, giving it a sacred canopy to make it legitimate. In this case, faith supported the cultural institution of slavery.

In the 1950s/60s, the civil rights movement led by Dr. Martin Luther King, Jr. provided a new <u>externalization</u> of integration to counter the established practice of segregation and racism. Rosa Parks and the Montgomery bus boycott, King's "I have a dream" speech, and the Selma/Montgomery march for voting rights were <u>objectivations</u> of the new reality. Many Americans no longer felt superior or inferior based on race, and the process of <u>internalization</u> meant a subjective change in the way we saw ourselves.

A key to this culture change is what happened to "the sacred canopy." King drew support from both black and white churches. I remember wearing a clerical collar along with hundreds of other clergy in the Selma march to demonstrate that churches and individuals of faith supported integration. King's movement drew on the Biblical image of Moses leading the children of Israel from slavery in Egypt to freedom in the promised land. He quoted the parables of Jesus where everyone was welcomed at the table of the Kingdom of God, particularly those who had experienced rejection by religious leaders. I felt I was part of an emerging generation of believers who sensed that God was calling us into a non-violent movement for justice. A new sacred canopy emerged, this time making equality and freedom legitimate in place of segregation and racism. As King emphasized over and over, his movement was not just lifting up black people or denying superiority to whites but changing the soul of America.

Faith impacts culture, and changes in culture set the agenda for new expressions of faith. As Franklin Woo notes in chapter four, Richard Niebuhr's <u>Christ and Culture</u> is a classic expression of five ways that Christian faith engages culture: Christ against culture, the Christ of culture, Christ above culture, Christ and culture in paradox, and Christ transforming culture. These different movements demonstrate that within one religion there can be many interpretations of faith because there is an ongoing dialectic bringing dynamic changes to both faith and culture. Another way to say this is to see that, as Berger says, human beings are world-building creatures and the faith/culture dialectic is at the heart of the process.

In this book we see the process of world building at work. Each chapter shows different ways externalizations are emerging in the world today and faith either provides or denies a sacred canopy for new objectivations. I see our writers as pioneers exploring new frontiers of culture. They bring their knowledge and sensitivity nurtured by faith in God to discern pathways to the future. We are invited to join them in their musings.

Jim Symons, Pasadena, October, 2013

ONE, BUT NOT THE SAME

Gary Demarest, Monte Vista Grove Homes, Musings, January 31. 2012

I'm grateful to Jim Symons for giving birth to this concept of Monte Vista Grove Musings. Hopefully, we launch, this evening, what will become occasional gatherings in which one of us retirees will present a theme growing out of our ministerial journey that might be relevant to us and to the church at large in contemporary culture.

Particular emphasis is to be placed upon the interaction of the Gospel and culture in the life of the contemporary church. While the Gospel calls the culture to conformity to the revealed will of God in Jesus Christ, the culture has always forced the followers of Jesus to re-think how they interpret and apply Scripture. The entire history of the church is the story of this interaction of Gospel with culture and culture with Gospel.

This presentation has been shaped significantly for me from the experience of being Co-moderator of the Theological Task Force on the Peace, Unity, and Purity of the Church appointed by the 2001 General Assembly.

We were directed "to develop a process and an instrument by which congregations and governing bodies throughout our church may reflect and discern the matters that unite and divide us, praying that the Holy Spirit will promote the purity of the Presbyterian Church (U.S.A.)."

This discernment was to "include but not be limited to issues of Christology, biblical authority and interpretation, ordination standards, and power."

The appointment of the Task Force grew primarily out of the continuing conflicts growing out of the issues surrounding the ordination standards for deacons, elders, and ministers, particularly those adopted in 1992, requiring chastity (abstention from all sexual behavior) by all ordained persons not living "within the covenant of marriage between a man and a woman."

Our work was presented to and adopted by the General Assembly in 2006, but, to no one's surprise, the controversies continue to trouble and divide us.

I give you this vignette, thus, as one who continues to muse upon the peace, unity, and purity of the church. And I am a "muser" who has become comfortable with the definition of musing as becoming "absorbed in thought, especially to turn something over in the mind meditatively and often inconclusively."

Like many of you, I stood long ago before God and a Presbytery and voluntarily subscribed to what are now nine ordination questions, or vows. Among them was my promise "to further the peace, unity and purity of the church."

Peace is not the absence of conflict, it is what we bring to each other in the midst of conflict. Unity is not achieved by seeking sameness of thinking or behaving, it is the love we bring to each other in our diversity. Purity is the most complex of the three involving both motivations and behaviors in every area of life. I have long since learned that we cannot produce or achieve peace, unity and purity. They are gifts of God to be used in the service of God. We can only FURTHER them.

Obviously, this vow only has meaning in the light of those that precede it. The starting point for our understanding and practice of ministry is not focused on the church or on ministry; it is centered in **JESUS CHRIST,** within the Trinitarian affirmation of Father, Son, and Holy Spirit. Our central confession has always been and must always be **JESUS CHRIST IS LORD!**

Whatever name, form, or polity a church adopts, to be the church of Jesus Christ is to identify ourselves as people who have chosen to respond to the call of God, trusting Jesus as Savior, and following him as Lord.

For centuries, these people have affirmed their identity in the classic Creeds, Catechisms, and Confessional statements of the churches. We gather around some of those statements in our Book of Confessions.

Whether we regard ourselves as conservative, evangelical, liberal, charismatic, progressive, or hybrid (will we ever run out of labels?), we do well to base our identity upon what have clearly emerged as the essential affirmations of our faith and practice: God the Father, Jesus Christ his only Son our Lord, the Holy Spirit, the holy Catholic church, the communion of saints, the forgiveness of sins, the resurrection of the body, the life everlasting.

While the classic Creeds do not refer to the inspiration and authority of the Bible, it is clear that the universal affirmation of the Creeds attests their faithfulness to the Scriptures of the Old and New Testaments.

Our identity as the church of Jesus Christ is inseparably rooted in our use of the Bible.

How we interpret and apply the Scriptures has and continues to be one of the critical issues in the interaction between the Gospel and culture. In United States history, it was the culture that drove what became the mainstream of the churches to change what had been their prevailing view of slavery, dividing the Presbyterian churches into two denominations at that time.

Ironically, it is our interpretations and applications of the Bible that impede our pursuit of the peace, unity, and purity of the church. We can't live without the Bible, but we seem to be unable to live together with it.

Some of you recall our conflicts in the writing of the Confession of 1967, and some left our denomination following its adoption. In fact, at least one new Presbyterian denomination was formed at that time.

In that Confession we affirm: **"The one sufficient revelation of God is Jesus Christ, the Word of God incarnate, to whom the Holy Spirit bears unique and authoritative witness through the Holy Scriptures, which are received as the word of God written. The Scriptures are not a witness among others, but the witness without parallel."**

Such an affirmation grows out of our interpretation of two passages in the New Testament found in Second Timothy and in First Peter:

"All Scripture is inspired by God *(theopnuestos)* **and is useful for teaching, for reproof, for correction, and for training in righteousness, so that everyone who belongs to God may be proficient, equipped for every good work" (2 Timothy 3:14-15).**

"No prophecy of Scripture is a matter of one's own interpretation, because no prophecy ever came by human will, but men and women moved by the Holy Spirit spoke from God" (2 Peter 1:20-21).

While these references to Scripture when they were written pointed to the Scriptures of the Old Testament, they have always been applied by the church to the writings of the New Testament as well, even though we have never come to universal agreement on the actual writings to be included in the Canon.

The term ***THEOPNUESTOS*** in the Timothy passage was coined by Paul and found nowhere else in the New Testament nor in Greek usage. It translates literally as "God-breathed," more traditionally "inspired by God." This word stretches our minds and imaginations.

I profess no way of knowing what actually transpired in this God-breathing process. On one hand there is divine initiative and activity. On the other is the actual literary production by particular individuals or groups.

When I read the Bible, I stand at the intersection of divine perfection and human imperfection, faced with mystery beyond my capability of understanding, much less defining or explaining. To me, holding this paradox of the divine and human nature of Scripture is not unlike my faith in the divine and human nature of Jesus. Explain it I cannot.

In recent years, right here at Monte Vista Grove, I have moved beyond the world of older persons and entered the world of older-older persons. I am both enjoying this process and finding it filled with meaning because of what I call the expansion of my **PMF: PARADOX MYSTERY FACTOR.**

I am increasingly aware that the things dearest to me and most basic to my living and dying are beyond my ability to fully understand as well as my ability to define or explain. And I'm becoming much more comfortable with ambiguity.

When I interpret and apply the Scriptures to life in the real world, I must be constantly aware that I do so in a community of faith, the entire body of Christ everywhere on this planet, that holds many differing interpretations and applications of them.

And I must resist the knee-jerk reaction to dismiss those with whom I disagree as not having as high a view of the authority of Scripture as I.

The Task Force to which I referred was not an affinity group of like-minded believers. Twenty of us were chosen BECAUSE OF our differences. We studied, prayed, and worked together for five years around the theme of furthering the peace, unity, and purity of the church.

Among other things, I learned that each of us, though coming from different personal, social, spiritual, and theological journeys shared a common and passionate commitment to Jesus Christ as Lord. Here we were one, but not the same.

I also learned that each of us shared a common and passionate commitment to the Bible as the word of God written. As we studied the Bible every time we gathered, it was increasingly clear that each of us took the Bible with shared seriousness. Here, it was most clear that we were one, but not the same.

I have come to the strong conviction that the ultimate meaning of the peace, unity, and purity of the church will be furthered by demonstrating that our oneness in Jesus Christ is best expressed through our differences, not through efforts to achieve and enforce sameness.

Without minimizing the significance of the importance of interpreting and applying our understanding of Scripture to issues raised by our culture, including those of human sexuality, marriage and family, abortion, immigration, wealth and poverty, we must bring an awareness to each other that neither uniformity nor unanimity has been the mark of any church tradition.

There have always been conflicts among the followers of Jesus as to the interpretation and application of the Bible in the personal, social, economic, and political areas of life. The history of the church has been that of continuing conflict and schism. The existence of hundreds of denominations and church groups, and the continuing formation of new alliances and splits is the reality we face.

I know of no greater challenge in this chapter of the Presbyterian Church (U.S.A.) than demonstrating to the world around us the power of Jesus Christ to make us one without requiring that we be the same.

I entered this Presbyterian family, not by birth but by choice. As the first graduate of Fuller Theological Seminary to be received as a minister in the PCUSA in 1952, having been ordained as a Baptist while in seminary, I was well aware that I was entering a denomination with significant conflicts, not the least of which was the ordination of women as ministers.

The first speech I ever made on the floor of a Presbytery was in opposition to the ordination of women as ministers. As I recall, my argument was quite Biblical, but obviously not very effective. I voted with the minority.

I could never have imagined then that somewhere down the road I would come to believe that such a change in ordination standards was being orchestrated by the Holy Spirit. I have voted with majorities later proven to be wrong, and I have voted with minorities later proven to right.

That's why my **PMF** (Paradox Mystery Factor) is so important to me as an older-older person.

Every challenge brought to the church by its culture, and God seems to have strange ways of working through unlikely channels, can be seen as a THREAT or as an OPPORTUNITY to discern what the Holy Spirit might be doing in the present.

One response to change to our traditional interpretation and application of Scripture is FIGHT AND FLIGHT. We defend our views, and if we lose the fight, we take flight. We direct more and more of our resources to the preservation of our position. The fights and flights continue, all to the loss of our identity and mission.

Living in a culture that is expanding in its diversity and becoming more intense in its polarization, I believe we have unparalleled opportunity to demonstrate the power of Jesus Christ to make us one without making us all the same.

For those who choose to continue in a denomination that has declined in numbers of churches and members some basic attitudes will be required.

WE NEED EACH OTHER

Of greatest importance is the recognition that we need each other because of our differences. Differences in Biblical interpretation and application are not something just to be tolerated. They must be welcomed and respected as essential to our growth. It is through these differences that we encounter the possibilities of change initiated by the Holy Spirit.

I realize now that across the years those with whom I have disagreed have sown more seeds for positive changes in my thinking and living than have those with who I have been in agreement.

I treasure the friendship and fellowship of those with whom I am very much alike. In small groups and covenant fellowships I have found and continue to find sustenance and strength for the journey.

I need affirmation, and I like mutual agreement, but I am more likely to experience growth in the depth and breadth of God's love by struggling with fellow believers with whom I have significant differences in our interpretations and applications of Scripture.

An essential premise of Presbyterian polity is that **"Presbyters are not simply to reflect the will of the people, but rather to seek together to find and represent the will of Christ" (G-4.0300c).**

If I were in active ministry today, I would stay loose with special interest groups based upon being like-minded on particular issues of the day. I would seek, rather, at every level of the church, to form groups based upon our differences, seeking to discover our oneness in Christ in the open sharing of those differences face-to-face in Bible study, sharing, and prayer. How else can we hope to "find and represent" the will of Christ?

We need each other the most at the points where we are in disagreement. The furtherance of the peace, unity, and purity of the church does not require the absence of conflict, nor can it be furthered by seeking uniformity.

ACCEPTING OUR FALLIBILITY

If we are willing to risk this frightening prospect of the fellowship of the unlike-minded, we must be open to a seismic shift in our need for certitude.

Each person must bring a full awareness of one's potential for error in the interpretation and application of Scripture.

Centuries before Rene Descartes well known declaration COGITO ERGO SUM (I think, therefore I am), the cornerstone of Renaissance and modern thought, Augustine declared: FALLOR ERGO SUM. The essence of being human is that we are fallible, capable of and prone to ERROR.

Don't we all agree that to err is human? Then why are so afraid of being wrong?

Having spent most of my adult life with the Bible as student, preacher, and teacher I have become aware of my proclivity to misuse, and even abuse Scripture, mostly driven by my insatiable need to be right, and the crippling fear of being wrong.

How natural it is for me to regard my interpretation and application of the Bible as normative. When I appeal most strongly to the authority of Scripture, I am most likely trying to establish the authority, not of the Scripture itself, but of my particular interpretation and application.

N.T. Wright indicates that Jesus did not say to his disciples, "All authority is given to the books you are about to write." He did say, "All authority is given to me." The right use of Scripture thus establishes the authority of Christ, not the rightness of my views.

Both this insatiable need to be right and this fear of being wrong must be identified and overcome. When I feel most right, I need be aware that I could be wrong. And when I fear most being wrong, I need be aware that I could be at least partially right.

Using the Bible as we stand at the intersection of divine infallibility and human fallibility, we do well to recall the observation of Abraham Lincoln in his Second Inaugural Address to the effect that when two people who worship the same God and use the same Bible come to differing conclusions, both of them can't be right; one could be right and the other wrong; both could be wrong; OR both could be partly right and partly wrong.

We fallible people need each other most precisely at the points where each of us may have part of the truth.

THE BIBLE ITSELF

The fact that the Christian community in its entirety has never achieved unanimity or uniformity in its interpretations and applications of Scripture says a great deal about the nature of the Bible.

There are opposing viewpoints and even contradictions within the writings of the Bible. Many of our differences rise out of the Scriptures themselves.

The arguments that I used in opposing the ordination of women as ministers were taken from the Bible. The arguments that I have long since used requiring the ordination of women are also taken from the Bible. (I'm ignoring the fact that arguments both for and against ordination itself can be found in the Bible).

Both sides of this issue are still being debated in churches in many parts of the world, including the United States, even in some Presbyterian denominations. The likelihood of resolving this conflict universally is remote as well as unnecessary.

On numerous social, cultural, theological, economic issues in the past and yet to arise, arguments on conflicting sides can be based upon some parts of the Bible. Opposing positions on some issues can be found even in a single writer such as Paul.

Hopefully, all of us with formal training in Hermeneutics learned that Biblical interpretation and application is complex and difficult. We have been called to a lifelong journey of faithful obedience to Jesus Christ in the interpretation and application of Scripture.

We can best further the peace, unity, and purity of the church by recognizing how difficult this is and how unlikely we will ever be of the same mind on every issue.

Far from being like an instruction manual for how to assemble the newest piece of furniture or an owner's manual on how to care for your new automobile, the Bible is a remarkably complex collection of writings from across the centuries, through which God still speaks to us today, even when we can't agree on what is being said.

RELATING TO PEOPLE OF THER RELIGIONS

Reflecting further upon the interaction between Gospel and culture, perhaps the most significant issues emerging for the churches in contemporary culture is how we regard and relate to people with other or no religious faith.

Here I share with you a conversation that has been going on within myself for most of my life. It began when I was in the eighth grade in Manhattan Beach.

One of my closest friends, Howard Jones, died of complications from a ruptured appendix, not uncommon in those years. It was my first encounter with the sudden death of a close friend.

That past summer, Howard and I had worked together on our Eagle Scout Merit Badges, and had even attended a Christian youth camp together. At the close of the camp I had responded to the invitation to accept Christ as my Savior. Howard did not. We continued to be best buddies, even though we never came to agreement about the faith.

Howard's funeral was the first I had ever attended. I neither remember the Pastor nor most of the service, but I have never forgotten leaving that service convinced that according to the Bible Howard was going to be tormented forever in hell's fires because he had not accepted Christ as his Savior.

That began a conversation that has been going on inside of me off and on for the past 75 years, and it never goes away fully. I find it difficult to relate the God that I am coming to know through Jesus Christ and the Scriptures as tormenting Howard eternally because Howard did not accept Christ as I had.

However, having said this, I'm well aware that this conversation has been going on for centuries among Christian thinkers and scholars. Gnostics, Marcionites, allegorists, typologists, and their kin have failed to develop a satisfactory resolution to this perplexing question of eternal punishment.

I think it fair to say that the majority view of Christians has been, and continues to be, that those who die with faith in Christ go to heaven for an eternity of bliss and those who die without such faith go to hell for an eternity of torment.

For all of my years as a pastor the conversation has taken on a global dimension as well.

My first ministry after Seminary began in 1950 at the University Presbyterian Church in Seattle, working with both High School and University students. For five years during the University year I was in a different fraternity or sorority with two or three students every Monday evening as dinner guests (jackets, ties, dresses, stockings and heels) followed by conversation in the living room about the Christian faith.

The question that arose most often in our presentations and discussions of the Christian faith centered on the fate and destiny of people who would die without ever having heard of Jesus, or of those of other religious faiths who did not affirm Jesus as Savior and Lord.

In retrospect, that question was different then that it is now. Few, if any, of those students, myself included, had ever had any significant personal contact with persons of other religions, even at the University of Washington.

That was the era of expansive "foreign" missions, and thousands of European and North American missionaries were passionate in their commitments to preach the Gospel to every people group on every Continent, to translate the Bible into every spoken language, and to make disciples of all peoples. That is still the mission of the Church as mandated by Jesus.

And that missionary passion and activity is now joined by growing ranks of Christian missionaries from Asia, Africa, and South America, the very people first reached by our missionaries. Some of them are now coming to North America to evangelize us!

The mandate of Jesus to his followers to "go into all the world and make disciples of all the peoples" has never been remanded. What has changed in our part of the world is that more and more of the peoples of the world have come to us. It is as though God has said to the North American churches: "I'll make it easier for you . . . I'll bring them to you."

People of all the religions of the world are among us in increasing numbers, and they are now building their temples, shrines, and houses of worship throughout the United States and Canada.

Add to the reality that we will be face to face with more and more people of other religions, the fact that there are significantly growing numbers of people in our communities who are identifying themselves as "spiritual but not religious." They profess belief in God but have little or no interest in organized religion. As a matter of fact, some of them are outright hostile to organized religion.

Are all of these people doomed to eternal torment by God unless they make a profession of faith in Jesus Christ as Savior and Lord? This question is not going to vanish. Clearly, there are many passages that can be used to support this view of eternal punishment.

Now we're back to the questions of how we interpret and apply the Scriptures. We must learn increasingly how to deal with the Scriptures in their entirety, not just with the parts of the Scripture with which we agree. Daniel Jenkins, world-class Christian missiologist, most recent book is entitled: "Laying Down the Sword." His subtitle is "Why We Can't Ignore the Bible's Violent Verses."

He works primarily in the context of Muslim-Christian relations in which some Christians are quick to label Islam as a religion of violence, while heralding Christianity as a religion of peace. The reality is that there are many passages in the Bible, as there are in the Koran that not only advocate violence but see it as ordered and blessed by God.

Every religion, including ours, has its Scriptures and parts of its history with chapters which cannot be interpreted and applied positively and convincingly.

It is in this context of people of other religions and no religion that we must learn to be faithful servants of Jesus and witnesses to God's unconditional love and mercy revealed in Jesus. I know of no greater challenge than doing this with love, energy, and intelligence.

Getting all of these people to join a church must not be a priority, nor must establishing that we are right and they are wrong. If I have done so in the past, I no longer will try to bring them to Christ by frightening them with eternal punishment, scaring the "hell" out of them.

I've long since become aware that I am unable to speak with certitude about the destiny of people who do not accept Jesus as I do. I suspect that God's love and salvation are much bigger than anything I can imagine. Who am I to judge what God can or cannot, may or may not do?

While John 3:16 is still one of my favorite verses: "God so loved the world that he gave his only son . . ." I find myself linking it always with John 3:17: "For God sent not his son into the world to condemn the world, but that the world might be saved through him." How God may ultimately accomplish this is way beyond my understanding.

This conversation inside of me prompted by my friend Howard's death and fueled by those conversations with students long ago will continue, and I no longer feel compelled to have all of the answers, much less do I claim to have all of the truth. God is so much bigger than I can grasp.

In many ways I feel like a child waiting for Christmas. I know the gifts have been made or purchased and wrapped, but I just have to wait until Christmas day to open them. I don't know how or when that day will come when I will finally be in God's presence. I can only wait for the full disclosure.

I'm still going to keep the conversation with Jesus and the Bible alive, as well as conversations with Moses, Joshua, Abraham, Paul, and the writers of the Gospels. I may need to include Mohammed and the Buddha in the conversation along with Origen, Marcion, Jerome, Augustine, and Pelagius. Of course I'll include the Reformers and even the Counter-Reformation Catholics and the Orthodox. I'll bring in the much younger folks such as Niebuhr, Barth, Brunner, C.S. Lewis, and Martin Luther King, Jr. And I mustn't leave out a lot of people with whom I disagree and many who I really don't like.

And I'm going to have a lot of differences with these folks, even to the point of serious disagreement. There are many Christians still opposed to the ordination of women, and some haven't given up on slavery or a flat earth.

I'm going to do my best to think and live "in obedience to Jesus Christ under the authority of Scripture, and continually be guided by our confessions," as I promised long ago.

I want to continue the conversations growing in my ability to listen, not only to people with whom I agree, but to those with whom I have disagreements. While I often enjoy the fellowship of those with whom I am in agreement, I am more likely to learn new dimensions of truth in the encounters with those with whom I am in disagreement.

Growing in my ability to listen I want to bring growing humility to every conversation, aware of my own fallibility and confronting my need to be right and my fear of being wrong.

As to the ultimate meaning of life and death, heaven and hell, I want to keep the resurrected Jesus central in the conversation, along with his teaching about heaven and hell, but I'm not going to ignore his teaching that also points to God's redemptive love for the whole world and for everyone who has ever lived on this planet, even before Moses and Abraham.

I will always keep John McKay in this conversation. For many years this former missionary to South America served as President of Princeton Theological Seminary. He became a treasured friend and mentor to me in his later years.

In what was my last conversation with him a few weeks prior to his dying, on a cold day in Georgetown he walked me to my car, bundled up in top coat and ear muffs. As I prepared to drive off, he said: "Remember, Gary, hold fast to Jesus Christ and stay loose with all the rest!"

I'm still just a little kid waiting for Christmas, and as I wait I treasure those words of Paul to the believers in Corinth:

"Love never ends: For we know only in part; but when the complete comes, the partial will come to an end. When I was an infant at my mother's breast I gurgled and cooed like any infant. When I grew up, I left those infant ways for good.

"We don't yet see things clearly. We're squinting in a fog, peering through a mist. But it won't be long before the weather clears and the sun shines bright! We'll see it all then, see it all as clearly as God sees us, knowing him directly just as he knows us.

"But for right now, until that completeness, we have three things to do to lead us toward consummation: trust steadily in God, hope unswervingly, love extravagantly. And the best of the three is love" (1 Corinthians 13:8-13, Peterson, <u>The Message).</u>

HISPANIC CHRISTIANS IN THE U.S. TODAY

Jane Atkins Vásquez, Monte Vista Grove Homes, Musings, May,15, 2012

The U.S. is home to 50 million Hispanics. They come from many backgrounds, differing cultures and various religious traditions. The great majority of Hispanics are Christians, living their faith as a system of belief and a moral compass. Recent writings on this subject include *Los Protestantes: An Introduction to Latino Protestantism in the United States* (2011) by Juan Francisco Martínez and his *Walk With the People: Latino Ministry in the United States* (2008). There are helpful studies by the Pew Hispanic Center, especially "Changing Faiths: Latinos and the Transformation of American Religion" (2007). Another interesting study, "Religion Matters: Predicting Schooling Success among Latino Youth" (2003) by David Sikkins and Edwin I. Hernandez comes from the Institute for Latino Studies at the University of Notre Dame. Also see the work by Ray Suárez, *Latino Americans: the 500 Year Legacy that Shaped a Nation* (2013). The terms "Hispanic" and "Latino" are used interchangeably here to refer to persons whose first language is Spanish or who are descended from those who originally spoke Spanish.

We begin with five basic scenarios:

- Hispanics were the first Christians in the Hemisphere.

- Latinos are a growing ethnic population of Christians in the U.S.

- Hispanics are diverse racially and culturally.

- Latinos are native born and immigrant.

- Hispanics are Roman Catholic, Protestant, Pentecostal and independent in their church affiliation.

We will look at the historical background, examine the role that immigration plays, look at the experience of Latinos in their faith, examine the challenges facing Hispanic Christians and meet a few of the religious leaders and theologians active today.

Hispanics/Latinos make up one of the fastest-growing ethnic groups in the United States. Most are Christians, but there is great diversity: Roman Catholic, Protestant, Pentecostal and independent church affiliation. Culturally and racially there is also diversity, with over 21 countries represented among the immigrant population and a variety of U.S.-born groups (Chicanos in the Southwest, Tex-Mex in Texas, Cuban-American in Florida, Puerto Rican on the island and the mainland, etc.). First we must examine the background of this complex group of people.

Hispanics were the first Christians in the Americas. Who are they and where did they come from?

For the last four centuries Latinos have lived in what is now the Southwestern U.S. They descend from the soldiers and settlers who came to the northern frontier of the Spanish American empire. Spain colonized the Americas, starting in 1492 with the arrival of Christopher Columbus and his little fleet of mariners. Although headed for the East Indies as part of an effort to build a commercial empire, Columbus quickly realized the potential of the Americas. Spain had just finished occupying the last Muslim state in Granada; the ethos of conquest dominated both church and society. Warriors gained fortune, fame and advancement in a feudal system based on ownership of land. Roman Catholicism was the official religion, the only accepted belief system and the powerful partner of the state.

After a dispute with Portugal over territorial prerogative, Spain was "awarded" most of the Americas by the Pope Alexander VI who enjoined the Spanish to convert the inhabitants to Christianity. To fulfill this objective, Spain sent missionaries to the "New World" along with the conquistadors and colonists. Franciscan and Dominican Friars, Jesuit priests and religious from other orders served first the Indian population and then the colonists from 1501 to 1821. Missions, or monasteries with dependent agricultural lands, were established in Florida in the early 16th c., in New Mexico in 1598, in Arizona in 1700, in Texas in 1719 and in California beginning in 1769.

Descendants of early Spanish colonizers from Texas to California settled in a region which was governed by Spain until revolution in the early 19th c. created an independent Mexico. Most of the people in the area were *mestizos,* or people of mixed race (Spanish, Indian, African and Asian) and Indian or Native Americans of many tribes or nations (Pueblo, Navajo, Apache, O'Odham [Papago-Pima], California Mission Indians, etc.).

English-speaking settlers established colonies along the eastern seaboard and sent out expeditions to explore and map the continent. Central to their thinking was the idea that the U.S. had a "Manifest Destiny" to control all of North America. As the U.S. moved westward, settlers migrated into Mexican Texas in the 1820s. The Americans were accepted by the Mexican government under three conditions: that they become Roman Catholic, that they become Mexican citizens, and that they not hold any slaves. However, Anglo residents of the deep South desired this territory because of its potential to expand plantations worked by slaves. Conflicts with Mexican authorities soon erupted and the Battle of the Alamo ensued. American immigrants created the "Lone Star Republic" which served Protestant Anglos from 1836 to 1845 when the area was claimed by the U.S.

From 1845 to 1848 fighting between the U.S. and Mexico raged from Texas to California to "the Halls of Montezuma" (Mexico City). When the Mexican-American War ended, Spanish-speaking people across the northern third of Mexico found themselves under a new, English-language government. "Manifest Destiny" was now completed: the U.S. was one nation from coast to coast.

The religious life of most "Mexican-Americans" was dominated by the Roman Catholic Church. There had never been enough clergy to serve the far-flung settlements, which depended on the laity to keep traditions alive. After 1848 Mexican priests and friars were replaced by U.S. Catholic religious, usually Irish, French or German and not Spanish-speaking. A new U.S. based Roman Catholic Church, which primarily served the elite, slowly developed in the Southwest. Except for one instance in a see which spread from Monterey to Los Angeles,

CA in 1873, Hispanic bishops were named to serve the Southwest only in the late 20th century.

Protestant missionaries came to the Southwest after the Mexican-American War. Denominational mission boards sent teachers, pastors and medical workers in the 19th and 20th centuries to evangelize and Americanize Latinos. Hispanics who became pastors served in a parallel system under supervision of Anglo administrators, even if they had received the same academic preparation as their Anglo counterparts. In contrast to mainline churches, Pentecostal denominations sent their members out to evangeliz family and friends as their churches grew in the 20th century.

Until 1900 Mexican American Protestants in the Southwest were mainly Methodists and Presbyterians, who made comity agreements to decide how the territories were to be evangelized. These two denominations established schools in areas where public education was available only in large cities. Presbyterians concentrated their work in northern New Mexico and southern Colorado, in Utah, in the mining towns of southern Arizona, in the Bay Area and in southern California.

The Presbyterians implemented the first school system with one or two room schools in the small villages of northern New Mexico and southern Colorado. When students completed their elementary education, they had the option of moving to boarding schools in Santa Fe, the Allison James for girls, or Albuquerque, Menaul School for boys. Upon high school graduation some earned a teaching certificate and others went on for higher education at church-related colleges or state universities. This system was financed through Presbyterian mission giving at the national level; most funds came from "back East." It contrasted with the Roman Catholic educational system which depended more on tuition and served mainly the elite.

One of the advantages of a Protestant education was learning to live within the dominant Anglo-American culture. Graduates from Protestant schools in New Mexico and Colorado more easily moved into the social, political and economic systems prevalent in their area. They became teachers, civil servants, legislators and business leaders.

Houses of Neighborly Service, small community centers, were a regular feature of Protestants within the Latino barrios of the Southwest. Missionaries were usually single women who organized classes in English as a second language, well-baby clinics, recreation for children and sewing circles for women. These centers were active from the early 20th c. until the 1970s and 1980s. Some later became independent agencies which continue to serve their communities as recreational and educational centers in neglected urban areas.

In the eastern U.S. the Hispanic population tends to come from the Caribbean. The Spanish-American War of 1898 resulted in the U.S. occupation of Cuba, Puerto Rico, Guam and the Philippines, islands that had been governed by Spain for 300 years. Anticipating U.S. occupation of Puerto Rico before the Spanish-American War, Protestant mission organizations made comity agreements to divide the island among the Baptists, Disciples of Christ, Methodists and Presbyterians.

Puerto Rico and Guam became permanent U.S. territories, while Cuba and the Philippines were independent, but dominated by the U.S. until the mid 20th century. Puerto Ricans have been U.S. citizens since 1917. Large numbers of Puerto Ricans immigrated to the Northeast, especially New York, and other parts of the continental U.S. over the years. Today there are more Puerto Ricans living in the continental U.S. than in Puerto Rico, largely because of employment opportunities. Roman Catholicism was the official religion of the island until 1898 but here, too, the church suffered from a lack of clergy to serve the people. Recently Protestantism has grown rapidly; today about 38% of Puerto Ricans are Protestants (Baptists, Disciples, Methodists and Presbyterian) and Pentecostal.

What role does immigration play for Latinos in the U.S.?

For the last 150 years, the Southwest has been impacted by Mexican immigrants who came to work, to escape the violence of civil war and revolution, and to join family already in the U.S. The border has long been home to stable bilingual communities, with daily crossings by both Mexicans and U.S. citizens. Until recently people crossed the border regularly to work, shop, go to school and visit family. For Hispanics the border is an inconvenience rather than a boundary.

Many Spanish-speaking people came to the U.S. in the early 1900s. Beginning in 1910 the Mexican Revolution forced thousands to flee from Mexico. In one case an entire Presbyterian congregation, led by the Rev. Jose Ibañez, came north and established a new church in Los Angeles. But eras of economic hardship, such as the Great Depression, caused more restrictive policies along the border. In the worst of times, U.S. citizens of Mexican descent were forcibly deported as part of the infamous "raids" conducted by state and federal authorities, and they continue today.

After the Cuban Revolution in 1959 immigration to the U.S. increased dramatically. Today there are nearly 1,500,000 Cubans living in the U.S. Most Cuban-Americans live in Florida, followed by New Jersey and New York. Most are vehemently anti-Communist and they exercise a disproportionately strong influence on U.S. politics regarding Cuba and Latin America. Some still hope to return to the island, while many regard the U.S. as their permanent home.

The wars in Central America in the 1980s forced people to leave their native lands in record numbers. One million Salvadorans emigrated,—500,000 to the Los Angeles area. Over 225,000 Guatemalans and 237,000 Nicaraguans also came to the U.S. as a result of the wars and economic hardship.

Hispanics in the U.S. today number about 50,000,000. Beginning in 2010 there has been a downturn in Hispanic immigration, partly due to the improved economy in Latin Americ (which pushes emigrants out) and the recession in the U.S. (which pulls immigrants into their country).

What are Latinos in the U.S. experiencing in their faith?

Hispanics contribute to the changing religious scene through changes in affiliation or denomination, in styles of worship and in expressions of belief. About 60% are Roman Catholics and 35% are Protestants or

Evangélicos[1]. Worship is increasingly charismatic or "renewalist," with lively music and a sense of celebration. Within the Roman Catholic tradition there is a "fiesta spirit" in worship. Mariachis, guitars and percussion instruments are used. The Pentecostal tradition includes speaking in tongues, divine healing and prophesying as part of the worship experience.

We have a clearer picture of Latino religious life as a result of the research conducted by the Pew Research Center. The Pew Research Hispanic Trends Project surveyed a national sample of over 4,000 people and collaborated with the Pew Forum on Religion & Public Life to discover more about the religious beliefs and practices of U.S. Latinos today. The result was a report called "Changing Faiths: Latinos and the Transformation of American Religion" published in 2007.

In the 1940s Lesslie Newbigin, British theologian and missiologist, aptly described the three branches of western Christianity (Roman Catholic, Protestant and Pentecostal) which emphasize different aspects of the faith. These three branches are represented in the Hispanic culture. For Roman Catholics, participation in the seven sacraments and veneration of the Virgin Mary are crucial. Protestants from historical or mainline traditions emphasize Bible study. Pentecostals rely on their personal experience of the Holy Spirit as they develop their faith and in the struggle between good and evil.

But some cultural traditions are present in all of these Christian branches and draw people together across religious differences. A girl's fifteenth birthday party or *quinciañera*, is observed by nearly all Latinos of Mexican descent. Saints' days can be observed by everyone, especially when they have a distinct cultural context. For example, St. John's Day on June 24th, observed with bonfires on the beach, is a special occasion for Puerto Ricans because it celebrates the patron saint of the island.

---

[1]   *Evangélico* and evangelical have different meanings, depending on the context. In the Spanish language the term *evangélico* usually means Protestant (as opposed to Roman Catholic). *Evangelical* in English usually refers to born-again Christians, often conservative and sometimes fundamentalist.

Generational changes in the churches are noticeable in Protestant and Pentecostal denominations. Ethnic churches are popular among first and second generation immigrants. The pastor is Hispanic, the congregation is largely Latino and worship is in Spanish. After the second generation, mixed churches are more popular. The pastor may be Hispanic or from another ethnic group, and is often bilingual. The congregation is a mixture of Latino, Anglo and other ethnicities. Worship is in English. Third generation and fully assimilated Hispanics often attend Mega-churches, where the congregation is a mixture of ethnicities. The general tendency is toward assimilation and participation in multiethnic English language congregations.

The Charismatic Movement broke into public consciousness in the U.S. in the 1960s. Today about 50% of all Latinos—Roman Catholic and Protestant—are Charismatics. These are Christians who practice the gifts of the Holy Spirit, but who are not members of historical Pentecostal denominations. Most belong to Catholic or Protestant denominations where gifts of the Spirit are not commonly emphasized. These are spirit-filled movements, with an emphasis on God's ongoing, day-to-day intervention in human activity. There is belief in supernatural phenomena such as speaking in tongues, miraculous healings, the gift of discernment, and prophetic utterances and revelations.

Most Latinos, regardless of their religious affiliation pray every day, attend a religious service at least once a month and have a religious object in their home, such as a cross or Bible. They may participate in cultural-religious events, such as a *quincianera* celebration, a saint's day-birthday or a Christmas observance such as *Las Posadas*.

Ministry among Latinos takes many forms, from very small store-front churches to very large churches with sophisticated audio-visual components. Within the mainline denominations there are churches more than 100 years old which still minister to descendents of their founding members. But even these congregations are changing as young people prefer to use English outside the home. Church leaders are challenged by the need to use Spanish with the older generation and English with the younger one.

What are the issues confronted by Hispanic Christians in the U.S.?

Issues facing Latino Christians in the U.S. clearly bring into focus the differences between this population and the dominant society. First and most important is immigration reform. The vast majority of Hispanics know someone who is personally touched by the uncertainty of living as an undocumented person. Until this issue is resolved, millions of Latinos will continue to live and work in the shadows, paying taxes and Social Security premiums for services they do not receive. Even the reporting of crimes and cooperation with police become problematic in the current situation. Closely related to immigration questions are civil rights issues. Some states have passed laws against "voter fraud" which make it difficult for Hispanic citizens to exercise their right to vote. Although there is little evidence of voter fraud, it is used as a reason to demand photo identification from a specific state office, which may be hard to obtain for those in rural areas. Voting by mail, same-day registration and expanded hours for voting have all been curtailed in efforts to limit minority participation. Racial profiling, or the assumption by police that any brown-skinned person is undocumented, is another civil rights problem for Latinos.

The values and ethics in today's society contrast sharply with those held by most Hispanics, for whom family is most important. Group solidarity, rather than individual achievement, is a prominent characteristic of Latino culture. "Where two can eat, three or four can eat" is a mantra commonly found: there is always enough to share with someone less fortunate or more dependent. The loving care given to children and the elderly are legendary, and make Hispanics the caregivers of choice as nannies and health care aides, whether in the home or in institutional settings. Teaching their own values, often at odds with those of the dominant culture, to their children is a continuing challenge.

Providing adequate educational opportunities for children and adults is another critical issue. Cut-backs in public schools directly impact the chances of Latinos. Increased class size, excessive testing and inexperienced teachers negatively affect outcomes for Hispanic children, who often start school with no knowledge of English. How best to teach these children and help their parents provide supportive learning environments are questions too often left unanswered. The demand for adult basic education continues to grow, while programs are eliminated to balance budgets.

Poverty, hunger, housing and employment issues challenge Latinos. The working poor, whether farm workers, hotel and restaurant employees or day laborers, are disproportionately Hispanic.

How do these concerns translate into theology?

Justo González, prominent Cuban-American Methodist writer and theologian, succinctly lists five theological issues:

- marginality,

- poverty,

- *mestizaje*,

- exile,

- solidarity.

Marginality means living on the outside of the dominant cultural paradigm. Poverty is coping with sub-employment, and sub-standard housing, schools and services. *Mestizaje* means being of mixed race, the result of the Spanish forcible conquest of Amerindians. Exile is living away from home or not having the same values as the majority culture. Solidarity is putting family and community first.

To address the need for a Latino-centered theology, González has helped found several organizations which bring together teachers, students and theologians: The Hispanic Summer Program, the Hispanic Theological Initiative and the Association for Hispanic Theological Education. These organizations are independent and yet maintain relationships with institutions of higher education and accrediting agencies.

The Hispanic Summer Program, started in the summer of 1989, was held for the first time at Andover Newton Theological School.

Over the years 1,000 Latino graduate students, and more than 100 non-Latinas/os, have taken nearly 150 courses at the HSP with 100 different Hispanic faculty. Sponsored by more than 50 seminaries of Evangelical, Roman Catholic, Protestant, Pentecostal and Orthodox denominations, the HSP is the only fully endowed Latino program in the U.S. One of the main goals of the HSP, to increase seminary graduation rates among Latinos, is being met.

The Hispanic Theological Initiative, another program González helped found, provides doctoral and post-doctoral fellowships at Protestant and Roman Catholic seminaries. The goal is to prepare more Latino teachers and writers as regular, tenured faculty in higher education. The resulting Hispanic teachers and writers are helping to "integrate" theological education for all groups, presenting Latino perspectives for an English-speaking as well as Spanish-speaking public. Since the program's inception in 1997, more than 50 individuals completed their Ph.D. studies and are working as faculty members, researchers and administrators.

The Association for Hispanic Theological Education (AETH, for its Spanish initials) has been created to serve seminary and Bible institute faculty and administrators. It provides a forum for the exchange of ideas and sponsors a biennial national conference. AETH publishes original theological and church-related works in Spanish written by today's Latino church leaders.

All of these organizations—the Hispanic Summer Program, the Hispanic Theological Initiative and AETH—have been awarded grants from the Lilly Endowment, Inc. and Pew Charitable Trusts as well as other funding agencies. This work is recognized for the consistent quality of the participants and for the leadership provided to the wider Latino religious community.

González is a prolific writer in both English and Spanish. He regularly produces Bible studies for the United Methodist Church. His works, *Mañana: Theology from a Hispanic Perspective* (1990) and, together with Ondina E. González, *Christianity in Latin America. A History* (2008) are only two of many books written for both Latino and English-language readers.

Hispanics, González says, see the world with non-innocent eyes. The Latino Protestant experience provides a unique lens through which to read the Bible. Latinos know that ideals and historical facts are not the same. "We are coming out of an age dominated by the twin myths of objectivity and universality." Our task is to "uncover the myths, discover the truth, recover the community."

Juan Francisco Martínez is associate provost and associate professor in the School of Theology of Fuller Theological Seminary. His research focuses on the history of Latino Protestants, Latino Protestant identity, ministry in Latino Protestant churches and the Latino Anabaptists in the U.S. and Latin America. A Mexican American from Texas and a Mennonite, he is the author of *Los Protestantes: An Introduction to Latino Protestantism in the United States* and many other studies of Hispanic Protestants.

Martínez sees Latino Protestants at a crossroads with points of encounter

- between North America and Latin America, between Euro-American Protestantism and Latin American Catholicism,

- between the first world and the majority world,

- between a dying Christendom and the vital new Christian expressions of the global south,

- between changing notions of the nation-state and the new transnational reality of migrant people,

- between the old racialized understanding of life together in the U.S. and the new intercultural relationships that are developing. *Protestantes*, p. 180.

Elizabeth Conde-Frasier is dean of Esperanza College of Eastern University, serving low-income Hispanics of northern Philadelphia. Formerly a tenured professor at Claremont School of Theology, Conde-Frasier chose to work at an institution that reaches students who have few opportunities for higher education. A Nuyorican, or native of New York of Puerto Rican descent, Conde-Frasier is an American Baptist. She teaches Christian education and writes on multicultural issues,

Latino theological education and the spirituality of the scholar. Her bilingual book, *Listen to the Children. Conversations with Immigrant Families* (2011), is about the one in five children who lives with an immigrant family. "The majority of these children will become lifetime residents of the U.S., and their presence will affect the basic institutions of society," she says (p. viii). What do these children need from their families? "Encouragement, expectations, role models, engagement and recognition" *Listen to the Children,* p. 34.

Virgilio Elizondo is a parish priest in San Antonio, Texas and professor at the University of Notre Dame. Writing on liberation and Hispanic theology, Elizondo celebrates the quality of *mestizaje* or mixed-race. Author of *Galilean Journey: The Mexican-American Promise; The Future is Mestizo: Life Where Cultures Meet* and other works, Elizondo identifies with the "least of these." These are the people who knew Christ: "the marginated of every socio-political group [are] most closely similar to the poor at the time of Christ . . . .""What human beings reject, God chooses as his very own." He encourages people to do theology: "Every Christian community [has] the privilege and the obligation of reflecting on its faith . . ."

Samuel Rodríguez is founder of the National Latino Christian Leadership Conference (NHCLC) which represents the majority of Latino evangelicals and Pentecostals. An Assemblies of God minister of Puerto Rican descent, Rodriguez and his wife, Eva, lead a church in Sacramento, CA. He is a member of the President's Advisory Council on Faith-Based and Neighborhood Partnerships. He speaks frequently on issues concerning Hispanics, especially education and immigration reform. Recognized as a leader, Rodriguez helps to set policies affecting Latinos within the context of faith-based initiatives.

Conclusion

We reviewed some basic scenarios about Hispanics in the United States:

- Hispanics were the first Christians in the Hemisphere.

- Latinos are a growing ethnic population of Christians in the U.S.

- Hispanics are diverse racially and culturally.

- Latinos are native born and immigrant.

- Hispanics are Roman Catholic, Protestant, Pentecostal and independent in their church affiliation.

Latinos bring strong faith and good values to the society in which they live, work and worship. The U.S. is fortunate that so many Hispanics choose to make their home here.

Selected Reading

Bannon, John Francis. *The Spanish Borderland Frontier.* Albuquerque: University of New Mexico Press, 1974.

Conde-Frasier Elizabeth, *Listen to the Childre: Conversations with Immigrant Families.* Valley Forge, PA: Judson Press, 2011.

Elizondo, Virgilio. *Galilean Journey: The Mexican-American Promise,* Maryknoll, N.Y.: Orbis, Maryknoll, 1983, 2000.

_____*The Future is Mestizo: Life Where Cultures Meet,* rev. ed. Boulder, CO: University of Colorado, 2000.

González, Justo. *Mañana: Theology from a Hispanic Perspective.* Nashville, TN: Abingdon, 1990.

González, Ondina E. and Justo L. González, *Christianity in Latin America: A History.* Cambridge, Cambridge University Press, 2008.

Martínez, Juan Francisco, *Los Protestantes. An Introduction to Latino Protestantism in the United States* Santa Barbara, CA: Praeger, 2011.

_____, *Walk with the People. Latino Ministry in the United States.* Nashville, TN: Abingdon, 2008.

Suárez, Ray, *Latino Americans: the 500 Year Legacy that Shaped a Nation.* New York: Celebra, 2013.

LIFE EXPERIENCES
IN THE GOSPEL OF JOHN

F. Dale Bruner, Monte Vista Grove Homes, Musings, October 16, 2012

Thank you so much for inviting me to share my life experiences with the Gospel according to Saint John. I have deeply enjoyed the almost three-decade immersion in this canonical masterpiece, and I hope that I can clearly share some of the main lessons learned in this engagement. Here is the main event in each Gospel chapter in a picture or two.

Chapter One. As you know, John's Gospel begins with the majestic Prologue, where God the Word became Jesus the creature in a kind of immense Cosmic-"V"-shape Descent. The Divine became human, the Infinite finite, the Supernatural natural, the Eternal temporal, the Absolute relative—the true God became a real human being. "The Word became flesh and moved into the neighborhood" (John 1:14 in Eugene Peterson's refreshing "Message" paraphrase. Jesus is a "homeboy," a "hoody"!). The most helpful practical description of John's use of "the Word" in his Prologue was given to me by a thoughtful laywoman in the discussion of an adult Sunday School class in The First Presbyterian Church of New Haven, Connecticut. She said, "What the audible 'word' is to the invisible 'thought' is what the historical Jesus is to the invisible God. We long to know what someone we care for is really thinking," she continued; "when that person puts his or her thoughts into words we finally learn the heart of the one we long to know. That's what the Great God did for us in Jesus of Nazareth," she concluded: "in Jesus, God put into an unforgettable 'Word' what God thinks of us and will do for us."

I remember the surprise I experienced when I first read (in a German newspaper editorial, unusually), and then confirmed by viewing, that in the American Western movie the hero always comes from outside town. I checked out "Shane," "High Noon," "Jeremiah Johnson," and "Unforgiven" to see if this was so. And sure enough, the hero was always an out-of-towner. (In "High Noon," however, Gary Cooper, the hero sheriff, is entering a horse-drawn carriage with his newlywed Grace Kelly, when he hears of "the bad guys" who are coming into town at noon; but as soon as he got outside town he said, "Amy; I've never run away from any man; I'm goin' back"; the carriage does a U-turn, and he comes back *into* town—because the hero of a Western movie, apparently, has always got to come from outside town! See how this "location situation" is the case in True Grit recently, too.) Ludwig Wittgenstein, the great twentieth-century philosopher, in an unintentionally theological "musing," put this outsider-insider "Incarnational" truth in Tractate 6.4312 of his *Tractatus Logico-Philosophicus*: "The solution [to] the riddle of life in space and time lies outside space and time." And in Jesus, the Church believes, this "solution" came inside space and time, classically. As John Donne put it in Ballad 15: "'Tis much that man was made like God before, But that God should be made like man much more."

In <u>chapter two</u>, which I call "The Wine and the Whip," we see Jesus "coming into his world" in two stories consecutively rich in "grace" and "truth." (In the Prologue in chapter 1. Jesus was twice described as coming "in grace and truth," vv. 14 and 17.) In deeply empathetic "grace," Jesus saves a wedding party from great shame by transforming the home's simple water into superabundant wine; then in passionate "truth," Jesus thoroughly rearranges the furniture in the Temple to teach that his grace is not indifferent to social and religious injustice. I think of "grace" as the wide horizontal beam on Jesus' Cross, and of "truth" as the deep and high vertical beam. Jesus is both, as this chapter vividly shows in two dramatic stories.

In <u>chapter three</u> (which begins with the last three verses in chapter 2), in Jesus' conversation with Nicodemus, we get a little "theology of evangelism." The chapter uses *"anthropos"* ("man" or "person") three times at the beginning of the story to teach us the Gospel's "anthropology": human beings, including even elevated Nicodemus, deeply need a new birth. The next major word in the chapter is *"pneuma"* ("Spirit"), used five consecutive times: the solution to the anthropological problem of sinful human beings is the gift of the transforming Spirit, given to believers in the water of Holy Baptism (v. 5). This invitation to Baptism with the Spirit is provided, we are then told, by the coming of the "Son" (*huios* in Greek, a word now used five times), who is sent by "God" (*theos*; used four times in all), like this: "God loved the world so much that he gave it his one and only Son, so that whoever entrusted oneself to him would not be ruined but would have deep, lasting life" (John 3:16). What chapter two taught about Christ's grace and truth in two consecutive stories, chapter three teaches in four consecutive nouns—"humans, Spirit, Son, and God."

John <u>chapter four</u>, Jesus' conversation with the Samaritan woman, is absolutely delightful, proceeding from the woman's rather rude opening responses to Jesus to, finally, the transformation of the whole town with her very earthy sermon: "Come & see a man who told me everything I ever did! You don't think this could be the Messiah, do you?!" One little introductory feature in the chapter particularly struck me: it is the text that says Jesus "found himself a place on the well because he was exhausted by the journey" (v. 6). In a Gospel so full of Jesus' Divinity, I treasure every reference, like this, to Jesus' ("exhausted") true humanity. We conservative Christians tend to overdo Jesus' Divinity and to underplay his humanity; more liberal Christians tend to stress Jesus' humanity so much that they make him "divinely" superhuman in their varied ways. I remember experiencing this difference dramatically. In December 1994, the cover story (in the now defunct Life Magazine) was entitled "Who Was Jesus?," and two consecutive contributors (one very conservative; the other very liberal) gave their compact answers to this question (p. 8). The Reverend Jerry Falwell, Pastor of the Thomas Road Baptist Church, Lynchburg, Virginia, had this striking sentence in his answer to the question: "He [Jesus] never once yielded to sin, nor was he at any time susceptible to injury or hurt or anything, mortal or otherwise." Did the Cross hurt? Did Peter's denials? Judas' betrayal? Was he "susceptible to exhaustion" here at the well? The next contributor to the Life article was by the Reverend F. Forrester Church, Unitarian Minister, and author of the book *God and Other Famous Liberals*. He wrote, "Ralph Waldo Emerson, a Unitarian, was a Spiritualist, as Jesus was. Emerson believed that Jesus was one deeply in touch with what Emerson called the 'over soul.' He thought Jesus divine precisely to the extent that we are [all] divine. The [only] difference being: Jesus recognized it [his divinity], and most of the rest of us don't." Is it true that human beings are divine but just fail to get in touch with this fact, whereas Jesus did? If we read the four Gospels at face value we will see both Jesus' true humanity ("My God, my God, why did you abandon me?") *and* his true divinity ("The Father and I are one"), without ruining the reality of either great fact.

In <u>chapter five</u>, which I call "Jesus' Divinity Sermon," Jesus is criticized for "making himself equal to God" by calling God "*My* Father" (v. 18). Jesus proceeds to teach that he can do absolutely nothing on his own but only by his being completely subject to the Father (vv. 19 to 30). The way Jesus spells out his relation with the Father in this chapter is the classic description of "how" Jesus is divine while still being entirely human, and has been treasured by the Church through the centuries. (A comparison of Jesus' Divinity Sermon here in John chapter 5 with Ralph Waldo Emerson's famous "Divinity School Address" at Harvard Divinity School, Sunday evening, July 15, 1838, is very revealing.)

<u>Chapter 6</u> is :Jesus'Bread Sermon," in which he first gives five-thousand hungry people real bread (and not "tracts"!), and then proceeds to teach, in three short sermons, how he is also humanity's True Bread from Heaven (consecutively: evangelical Bread, vv. 25-40; ecumenical Bread, vv. 41-51; and eucharistic Bread, vv. 52-58). My favorite single passage in the chapter is in verses 28 and 29 where the crowd asks Jesus what *they* should *do* in order "to be doing the works of God." Jesus' reply is excitingly evangelical: "This is the work of *God*," Jesus replied (notice *whose* "work"!): "that you *believe* in the One whom he sent, for on this person the Father has placed his seal of approval." We humans long to know what should we *do* to be pleasing to God; and the deep Johannine (and Pauline) answer to this most pressing of human questions is this: "believe in the One the Father sent," i.e., Jesus. Simple believing in (trusting) Jesus Christ, the Son whom the Father sent into the world he loves so much, is the "work"—"of *God*"—that Jesus wants us humans to "do." I love the *sola fide* ("faith alone") answer of Jesus; I also love the fact that the one who "works" this believing in his Son "into us" is God himself; and I like the fact that in the whole Gospel of John the verb "believe" is never preceded by an adjective or an adverb (like "*sincerely* believe," or "*deeply* believe," or the like). The moment we add an adjective or adverb to the Gospel's "believe" we add our "good works," and believing ceases being *sola*, sole, or simple. That *the* way to God the Father is (simply!) believing his Son is absolutely thrilling,

life changing, and doing-creating, and wherever this *solus Christus, sola gratia, sola fide* fact has been rediscovered in the Church there has been reformation, renewal, revival, and re-doing.

I call John chapters 7 and 8 "Jesus' Controversy Sermons" because they are packed with often bitter arguments against Jesus by his major opponents, and they are accompanied by Jesus' deep and often mysterious responses. There is a single little "pool of relief" about two-thirds of the way into each chapter. In chapter 7, at verses 37-39, we read: "On the last great day of the Festival, Jesus took his stand and cried out saying 'If anyone is thirsty, let that person come here to me and drink away! The person who entrusts oneself to me, as Scripture says, "Out of that person's innermost being will come flowing rivers of living water." 'He meant by this water," John goes on to explain, "the Holy Spirit, who was just about to be received by those who trusted Jesus. You see, the Spirit had not yet been given because Jesus had not yet been glorified." *Solus Christus, sola gratia, sola fide* again! In chapter 8 at verses 30-32, Jesus promises those who had believed in him amidst all opposition: "If you will now make your home in My Word, then you will be my disciples in reality. And I promise: you will come to know the very Truth, and this Truth will set you free." These two sets of three verses in chapters 7 and 8 are filled with the most exciting promises for the Church in the entire Gospel of John.

I call John chapter 9 "Jesus' & the Blind Man's Sermons" and give the chapter the sub-title: "How the Man Who Always Tells the Truth Honors Jesus." It is the blind man who does most of the talking in the chapter, and every single time he opens his mouth he says nothing but the truth, even when it could hurt him—even to Jesus near the end of the chapter. I like this once blind man a lot. His famous reply to his Pharisee accusers (who threaten him, we recall, with the words: "Give glory to God, fellow; we know that this man [Jesus] is a sinner!," verse 24), deserves special attention. He does not say, "Oh no, he is not a sinner!," because the man barely knows his healer; and besides, he has been blind from birth. He will never lie. Nevertheless his answer to their threat is classic: "Whether the man [Jesus] is a sinner or not, I do not know. I know one thing: I am a blind man and now I see" (v. 25). Near the end of the chapter, Jesus "finds" the once-blind-man (who, incidentally, has just been "thrown out" of the Pharisees' meeting because of his audacious representation of Jesus, v. 34). Jesus asks him, "Do you believe in the Son of Man?" The man won't even lie to Jesus and say "yes, I sure do!" He has as little knowledge as we do of the meaning of this most mysterious and personal of all Jesus' self-designations—"The Son of Man." So he cannot honestly say, "Of course," or even a humble "Yes." Instead, typical of him, he asks Jesus an honest question, and you can tell he trusts this Voice that healed him a few hours earlier: "Who is he, sir, so that I can believe in him?" (By the way, Jesus' slightly oblique question of the man, "Do you believe the Son of Man?," is a dramatic example of the famous dictum about Jesus' way with people: "Jesus always *gives people just enough of himself* to make faith possible; but he *hides just enough of himself* to make faith necessary.") Jesus answers the man's honest question ("Who is he, sir, so that I *can* believe in him?"): "You have just seen him & he is the one who is in conversation with you." To which the man climactically replies, "I believe, Lord"; and the Evangelist John immediately adds "and the man *worshiped* Jesus" (vv. 35-38). The artistry of this whole ninth chapter has often been praised. Preachers and teachers of the Gospel of John will almost unanimously report that this ninth chapter (along, often, with chapter 4's Samaritan Woman and chapter 11's Lazarus) is the easiest passage in the entire Gospel to present because it is so alive with drama.

In chapter ten, which I call "Jesus' Good-Shepherd Sermons," we see Jesus seeking a Christocentric Church. Jesus begins his sermon by warning his sheep of "Otherwayers"—that is, people who come into the sheepfold of the Church preaching "other ways" to Life beside Jesus Christ himself, who alone is the One Gate to Life. In reading this chapter one is reminded of the famous "Theological Declaration of Barmen" (1934), where the German Confessional Church publicly opposed the state-glorifying German Church, and in which John's Gospel especially and this tenth chapter of the Gospel with its blazing Christoexclusivity, particularly, are put to good use. Here is the First Thesis of Barmen, with its famous Introduction (I have underlined the words that I believe are particularly important):

"In view of the errors of the 'German Christians' of the present Reich Church government, which are devastating the Church and are also thereby breaking up the unity of the German Evangelical Church, we confess the following evangelical truths:

"[Thesis] 1. *'I am the Way, and the Truth, and the Life; no one comes to the Father but by me'* (John 14:6). *Truly, truly, I say to you, he who does not enter the sheepfold by the Door but climbs in by another way, that man is a thief and a robber . . . . I am the Door; if anyone enters by me, he will be saved'* (John 10:1, 9).

"[Affirmation]: *Jesus Christ, as he is attested for us in Holy Scripture, is the one Word of God, which we have to hear and which we have to trust and obey in life and in death.*

"[Condemnation:] *We reject the false doctrine, as though the Church could and would have to acknowledge as a source of its proclamation, apart from and besides this One Word of God, still other events and powers, figures and truths, as God's revelation.*"

I call John chapter 11 "Jesus' Lazarus Sermon," where Jesus shows us in his Raising of Lazarus, here inside Jesus' public ministry, that he can even conquer our final enemy—death itself. I collect in my Bible's opening and closing blank pages the deep remarks on the subject of death that I encounter in the course of my reading. Here are a few of my favorites: "If *death* is the strongest negation we know [in] human life and [of] life's meaning, then the Easter Faith [in Jesus' historical Resurrection] is the strongest 'No' ever directed at this negation" (Josef Blank, *John*, 1981, p. 136).

Luther can even be humorous about the subject, as we see in one of his sermons on the Gospel of John to his people in Wittenberg: "Many great men lost their minds because they could not find out where one goes when departing this life. Hence the proverb: 'I live, How long I do not know; Must die, But know not when I'll go; Pass on, But know not where 'twill be. My cheerfulness surprises me'" (*Luther's Works*, American Edition, vol. 22, p. 305, to John 3:11-12).

Then these thoughtful remarks by a thoughtful secular writer: "One reason [why we cannot seem to learn to die], of course, is that death is the one great adventure of which there are no surviving accounts;

death, by definition, is what happens to someone else. Empiricism falters before death. Yet [death] is more certain than love and more reliable than health." Pico Iyer, "Death Be Not A Stranger," *Time Magazine* (August 8, 1994), p. 68. (Incidentally, is not Jesus' Resurrection a strikingly singular "surviving account" of death?)

"With the revelation of the Risen One the seeking, not only of the disciples but the seeking of all human beings, reached its actual goal." Udo Schnelle, *Johannes,* p. 303.

I call John chapter 12 "Jesus' Valedictory Sermons" because here he ends his public ministry, immediately prior to his Upper Room private talks with his disciples (chapters 13-17) and prior to his subsequent Passion (chapters 18-21). I call Jesus' final sermon in this final public-ministry twelfth chapter "Jesus' Sermon Cry of Transparency (His Last Words to the World)," because in this chapter Jesus teaches the very important doctrine of his transparency to God the Father, one of the two or three most important teachings of the entire Gospel according to John. Jesus does not claim to be the end himself. His whole ministry is to bring the world his Father, the Living God. Listen to Jesus' ringing conclusion: *"Then Jesus cried aloud: 'Whoever believes in me believes not in me but in him who sent me. And whoever sees me sees him who sent me . . . . I have not spoken on my own, but the Father who sent me has himself given me a commandment about what [I am] to say and [about] what [I am] to speak. And I know that his commandment is eternal life. What I speak, therefore, I speak just as the Father has told me"* (verses 44-50). The End of Jesus' Public Ministry.

Eugene Peterson, humorously but effectively, calls John chapters 13-17 "The Jesus Seminar," where Jesus famously talks in an upstairs room exclusively to his disciples in a kind of graduate course in theology. I find Jesus in these five chapters to be teaching disciples, respectively, *themselves* in chapter 13; *The Father* in chapter 14; *The Son,* himself, in chapter 15; *The Holy Spirit* in chapter 16; and finally, I call chapter 17, in which Jesus prays the entire chapter, *The Lord's Lord's Prayer.* Let me explain each chapter in turn.

Chapter 13. I call the opening chapter of Jesus Upper-Room Discourse "Jesus' Footwashing Sermon," because here he teaches his disciples during his washing of their feet, in summary form, the three most important truths they must remember about themselves (Let yourselves be loved by me; Be servants to one another; and Be careful about yourselves). The first truth impresses me most. Peter "humbly" (!) rejects Jesus' Footwashing (*"Are you washing my feet?!"*). After some more clumsy "Peterisms," Jesus, in an unforgettable rebuke, teaches Peter, and so all future disciples the single most important of all theological *and* personal truths about ourselves: *"Peter, if I can't wash your feet, you can't have my fellowship"* (v. 8), which, translated, means, "Dear Disciple: If you won't let me forgive you—if you won't accept my seemingly undeserved love—I don't know how you are going to make it." Our accepting Jesus' gracious and undeserved accepting of us is the foundational personal truth of the Gospel, and Jesus' Footwashing encounter with Peter at the beginning of the chapter beautifully teaches this wonderful Gospel truth.

After this foundational teaching at the beginning of the thirteenth chapter, my second favorite passage in the chapter is the Gospel's first reference to The Beloved Disciple, in verse 23: *"One of Jesus disciples— the one whom Jesus loved—was reclining right next to Jesus* [literally, *"was at the bosom of Jesus," en to kolpo tou Iesou].*" This disciple will appear seven times in this second half of the Gospel (chapters 13-21). What I find the Evangelist John saying about the Beloved Disciple here is this: Jesus, whom John at the conclusion of his Prologue to the Gospel wrote, *"is back at the bosom of the Father"* (1:18: *eis ton kolpon tou patros*), will be most accessible to the future Church by her coming to Jesus through the disciple who is introduced here *"at the bosom of Jesus."* In short, Dear Church: If you want to come to the Jesus, who is at the Father's heart, the most dependable route is to come to him through the Disciple who is at the heart of Jesus. (Mathematically: Jesus:God::The Beloved Disciple:Jesus.) In short: The best way to Jesus is through the Gospel of John! I honestly believe that this is what John is suggesting in his pictorial language; verse 23 is a subtle internal advertisement for John's Gospel.

The Beloved Disciple, as mentioned, will appear seven times in the second half of the Gospel and, interestingly, in five of those seven times he is depicted with Simon Peter, the traditional oral source behind Mark's Gospel (believed to be the earliest of all the Gospels).

And all five times that Peter and the Beloved Disciple are reported together in John, the Beloved Disciple does something superior to Peter. For example, here, immediately after this first reference to the Beloved Disciple, we read that Peter leaned across the table and asked the Beloved Disciple to ask Jesus, "Whom does Jesus mean when he said 'One of you disciples is going to betray me'?" Which John then asks, and Jesus answers him (verses 24-26). The important detail to notice here is that the Beloved Disciple is closer to Jesus than even Peter, who has been traditionally believed to be the person closest to Jesus. (Is this carefully crafted scene another subtle internal advertisement for this Gospel?)

In John 14, "Jesus' Father Sermon," the Church's favorite text has usually been Jesus' regal response to Thomas' honest question (*"Lord, we don't know where you are going. So how can we know the way there?,"* v. 5). Just a little earlier we heard Jesus' answer to Thomas' honest question in the opening Scriptural citation in the Barmen Declaration against Hitler: *"Jesus said to [Thomas]: 'I am the Way [there], and the Truth [that will lead you there], and the Life [that will empower you to get there]. No one comes to the Father except through me"* (v. 6). This is perhaps the single most impressive Christocentric text in all of Scripture. It has repeatedly contested every attempt by the Church to say that there are other ways to God beside Jesus.

In John 15, "Jesus' Son Sermon," Jesus invites his disciples to "abide in me," which I translate "make your home with me." Exactly *how* we "make our home" with Jesus is left to the conscience of each disciple. Jesus gives no techniques. I think the simplest meaning is "spend some time with me please." The major way we do this is probably by going to Church on Sundays to hear him talk to us in His Word; to talk with him in prayer; to sing to him with his people; and to eat his meal with his people and him. Then each disciple (and family) determines privately how to "make one's home with him."

Because I am a slightly "driven" person, who needs a plan to get things done, I have devised what I call "The Gospel House" as the way I hope I can "Make My Home with Jesus." I read just a chapter of his New Testament in the morning and then seek, simply and briefly, to pray over (to respond to) the main word(s), phrase(s), or sentence(s) in the chapter (the parts, usually, that I underline as I read) that Jesus spoke to me that morning in the reading. In the hope that this might be helpful to some, here is how I divide my Gospel House by months, proceeding through the New Testament, chapter by chapter, book by book (reading, for example, Matthew chapter one on January 1ˢᵗ, chapter 2 on January 2ⁿᵈ, and so on through the month):

Jan	Feb	Mar	Apr	May	Jun	Jul	Aug	Sep	Oct	Nov	Dec
Matt	Mark	Luke	John	Acts	Rom*	Cor*	GEPC*	TP*	HJ*	PJ*	Rev

(*"Rom" = "Romans"; "Cor" = I, II Corinthians; "GEPC" = Galatians, Ephesians, Philippians, Colossians; "TP" = I, II Thessalonians, I, II Timothy, Titus, Philemon; "HJ" = Hebrews, James; "PJ" = I, II Peter; I, II, III John, Jude; "Rev" = Revelation.)

John 16 gives us Jesus' most extended teaching on the Holy Spirit (in nine connected verses, 7-11 and 12-15; see the earlier brief references to him in 14:16-17, 26 & 15:26) and so I call the chapter "Jesus' Spirit Sermon." Jesus' favorite word for the Holy Spirit in this chapter as well as in the two preceding chapters is *ho Parakletos*, "The Paraclete." Traditionally the two words have been translated as "The Comforter" or "The Advocate." The words, literally, mean "The Called" (*ho kletos*) "Alongside" (*para*, compare our English word "parallel"). Hence I am inclined to think that John's Jesus wants us to think of this Person as the One who is called alongside us to help and to guide us. I am presently translating the words as "The Encourager." But I am open to better translations. I especially like the Encourager's Christocentricity. Notice across all three chapters (14-16): *"But the Encourager, the Holy Spirit, whom the Father will send <u>in my name</u> [!], will teach you everything [you need to know], and will remind you of all that <u>I</u> [!] have said to you"* (14:26). *"When the Encourager comes, whom <u>I</u> will send to you from the Father, The Spirit of Truth who comes from the Father, he will testify on <u>my</u> [!] behalf"* (15:26).

And then most extensively in our sixteenth chapter "Jesus' Spirit Sermon", Jesus teaches us: *"When [The Encourager] comes, he will prove the world wrong about what is wrong, wrong about what is right, and wrong about who won. Wrong about what is wrong, because [the main wrong is that] they do not believe in me [!]; wrong about what is right, because [the main right is that] I am going to the Father . . . ; and wrong about who won, because [in fact] the ruler of this world has been soundly condemned . . . . When the Spirit of Truth comes, he will guide you into all the truth; for he will not speak on his own, but will speak whatever he hears, and he will declare to you the things that are to come. He will glorify me [!], because he will take what is mine [!] and declare that to you"* (16:8-15). I have liked to think of the Holy Spirit as "The Shy Member of the Trinity" in this sense: In John's depiction of the Encourager Spirit, he constantly points away from Himself to Christ. I don't think that our Christian meetings are necessarily filled with the Spirit when we talk a great deal about the Spirit. Such meetings are "off center." I believe that John's Gospel is trying to teach us that the more Christ centered our meetings are the more Spirit filled they are. (To depict this teaching graphically in class situations I have liked to draw a picture of Jesus on a portable white-board and then to stand *behind* the board with my finger pointing insistently, in front of the board, to the depicted Christ, and to say from behind the board: "This is the Ministry of the Holy Spirit: To point to Christ and not to Himself.")

In chapter 17 Jesus prays the entire chapter. I like to call this chapter "*The Lord's* Lord's Prayer" because in it, as in The Lord's Prayer that Jesus taught his disciples (in Matthew 6; see the only slightly different Luke 11), there are exactly six petitions. And our Lord's six Petitions almost exactly parallel the six Petitions he taught his disciples to pray. (The only exception is Jesus putting the sixth Petition in third place— perhaps in order not to end his prayer with "the Evil One," from whom the disciple prays to be delivered at the end of their prayer. Jesus would prefer to end his prayer here for his disciples with this petition for their presence with him in the great future world.)

I will append The Lord's Prayer (Matthew 6), The Lord's Lord's Prayer (John 17), and The Children's Catechism Lord's Prayer at the end of this document so that readers can see the six parallels. Let me give these brief alerts: Notice how at the very beginning of each prayer the readers are referred both to the Father and to heaven. Notice that the glory of the Father is the shared point of the First Petition, and that in typically Johannine fashion, this occurs through the glorification of the Son whom the Father sent to make Himself known. In the Second Petition the Father's Kingdom comes most perfectly to earth, in John's hearing, when Jesus' disciples are kept in the Name (*"I Am"*) that the Father gave to His Son (i.e., kept in Christcenterdness); for when the Son is honored, the One who sent Him is honored. In the Third Petition, as suggested above, Jesus (or John) may have taken Jesus' Sixth Petition to the disciples and placed it here in Jesus' prayer. But in both prayers, disciples are to be concerned about their struggle with the Evil One at least one-sixth of their time in prayer. (In a way, the Third Petition in both prayers is saying the same thing in directly opposite ways: *"Thy Will Be Done"* is said in another way when we ask that the Devil's will *not* be done: *"Please keep us from the Evil One."*)

In the Fourth Petition that Jesus gives his disciples to pray (in Matthew), they are taught to pray for earthly bread—Jesus is not indifferent to earthly realities (see his Feeding of the Five Thousand with real bread in all four Gospels). The Church has always loved the earthiness of Jesus. True, as Jesus learned in his Temptations, *"Human beings do not live by bread alone"* (Matthew 4:4), but the biblical texts and reality do not say that human beings do not live by bread at all. John's Gospel apparently believes that with the prayer for real bread engraved into two Gospels (Matt 6:11; Luke 11:3), that Jesus can be heard to be praying in his fourth petition for the deepest bread of all for his disciples: *"Please sanctify them in the Truth; your Word is Truth"* (v. 17). Disciples have been taught by Jesus to hunger most deeply of all for Truth; and it is encouraging to learn from Jesus here that the deepest Truth of all is present in the world in God's Word, whom the first chapter of this Gospel taught us is Jesus himself (1:1-18). And the Church has been convinced through the centuries that "the *earthly* Word" about this *"Divine-Human* Word" is the canonical Scriptures. The Fourth Petition of The Johannine Lord's Lord's Prayer, therefore, will drive its petitioners to long for the biblical Gospel.

The Fifth Petition in both Prayers (The disciples' and Jesus') teaches that our forgiveness of each others' sins *and* the prayer for the oneness of Jesus' earthly disciples are complementary petitions—the one feeds the other. May we Christians be forgiving, particularly with one another, and be so united with one another in the Church that the world will be struck by our oneness and so come to believe and know that God the Father, and no one else, sent Jesus the Son, and no one else, to teach the world the True God.

Finally, in the last Petition of the earlier Lord's Prayer, disciples are taught to pray for victory over future Temptation and deliverance from the Devil. John heard Jesus pray in Jesus' Sixth Petition that disciples would be brought to Him in His eternal glory. I hear this Johannine Petition teaching us disciples to seek victory over the fear of death and to have the Christian Hope. Christian Faith and Christian Love mean a great deal to me; but I must confess that I do not dwell enough on The Christian Hope, and so this final Petition in John convicts me.

I am deeply grateful that we have both The Lord's Prayer *and* the Lord's own "Lord's Prayer" to teach us how to pray.

In chapter 18, the beginning of Jesus' Passion Experience, which I call "Jesus' Court Sermons," Jesus says three times in the first story, *"Ego eimi," "Ego eimi," "Ego eimi": "I Am [he]," "I Am [he]," "I am [he],"* again and again to his arresters (vv. 5, 6, and 8), and in the process actually "knocks them over" (v. 6), teaching readers again, surely, the power of Jesus' Person and Word (see also Psalm 27:2 & 35:4). Peter, on the other hand, says repeatedly in the chapter's subsequent stories, *"ouk eimi," "ouk eimi," "Not me, Not me"* (vv. 17, 25, and see the report of his third denial in v. 27), providing a striking contrast. I am impressed, particularly, by Jesus' poise before Pilate in Jesus' Roman Trial, and especially by the climactic exchange between the two in their first meeting (vv. 37-38). Jesus tells Pilate: *"The whole reason I was born and the whole reason I came into the world was this: to bear witness to the Truth. Every person whose life is rooted in the Truth listens to my voice."* To which, famously, Pilate replies, *"What is Truth?"* We would love to know Pilate's tone of voice when he asked this question: cynical? sincere? dismissive? questing? Certainly everything depends, does it not?, on *how* Pilate asked and meant this most fundamental of human questions? In street talk, believers are tempted to answer Pilate's question with the rejoinder, *"In your face, Pilate!"* The man facing Pilate that very moment, and to whom Pilate specifically directs his question, is, in fact, Christians believe, God's flesh-and-blood *answer* to Pilate's question (and ours) about truth—and it is present before him *in person.*

In chapter 19 Jesus dies on the Cross, famously, with a single Word (v. 30): *"'Finished!' [tetelestai], and then he bowed his head, and handed over the Spirit."* The reader is moved to ask "<u>What</u> is finished?!" And the Gospel-reading Church through the centuries has been inclined to respond, "The Revelation of God to the World" and "The Reconciliation of the World with God." The immediately following words, *"he bowed his head,"* are the words used in Homer's *Iliad* to indicate a deity's affirmation of his or her preceding words. For example, Thetis pleads with Zeus: "Promise me now this thing in very sooth and *bow thine head thereto,* or else deny me, . . . that I may know full well . . . ." Whereupon Zeus replies, "[C]ome, *I will bow my head to thee, that thou mayest be certain,* for this [bowing] from me is the surest token among the immortals; no word of mine may be recalled, nor is false, nor unfulfilled, whereto I bow my head" (A.T. Murray's *Loeb Classical Library* translation, Book I, lines 514-27, emphases added).

Johann Sebastian Bach knew this Greek idiom and so, immediately after Jesus' last cry and symbolic deed, *"'Finished!' And he bowed his head,"* Bach wrote Aria 60 in his *Saint John Passion* (in my translation, with emphases added):

> "My priceless Savior, let me ask this question:
> When Cross-nailed you are so diminished,
> Say you yourself that *all* is *'finished'*?!
> Have I, in fact, from *death* been freed?
> Through your despair and desolation
> am I *myself* assured salvation?
> There *all the world's* salvation, too?
> In your deep pain you speechless bled,
> yet when you just now bowed your head,
> it seems, in fact, that 'Yes' you said."

In <u>chapter 20</u>, "Jesus' Resurrection-Mission Sermons," we learn how the Risen Lord revealed himself to his first disciples. When Peter and the Beloved Disciple run to the tomb, after Mary Magdalene's terrified report of what she thought was Jesus' stolen body, it is so interesting to see how, three different times, the Evangelist stresses the Beloved Disciple's outrunning Peter (vv. 4, 6, and 8), a theme we have picked up in every other reference to the two disciples together. This repeated theme suggests to me again that the Beloved Disciple, the putative source of this Fourth Gospel, is saying to the hesitant Church: "Please put me in the Canon. Peter's Synoptic-Gospel Mark is very good indeed; but whenever we were together, I consistently was just a little superior." Is this "evangelical-appeal" interpretation of our texts too creative or, perhaps, even irreverent? I hope not. It is what I discover from the five-fold Beloved Disciple and Peter juxtapositions in this Gospel. (Historically, the early Church was hesitant to put John in the Canon at all because the newly emerging super-spiritual Gnostic "Christians" used John in their super-spiritual ways.)

My single favorite verse in this twentieth chapter, recording the first human meetings with the Risen Lord, reads like this. The grieving Mary Magdalene has just spoken to the person she thinks is the gardener, and then she turns her back, whereupon Jesus addresses her by name (v. 16): *"Jesus says to her 'Mary [Mariam]!' The woman turned and says to him in Hebrew, 'Rabbouni!' (which means, 'Teacher!')."* I call this meeting "The Turn." Can we even imagine the emotions present in this single verse? When she makes her 180 degree turn to Jesus, I think to myself that in the one-to-two seconds that this turn took, the world shifted slightly on its access, and history moved from B.C., "Before Christ" to "A.D.," "In the Year of Our Lord." At one moment, Mary is experiencing the deepest grief of all—the death of a loved one; in the very next moment, as she made her world-historical Turn, she is experiencing the deepest human joy of all—the conquest of the final enemy, Death. Can one imagine the "rush" of that two-second Turn? Jesus' one-word "Mary" is the shortest sermon in The Gospel of John and, indeed, in the entire Bible. But with that one word—a personal name—everything is, indeed, now even subjectively (and not only objectively) "finished!" Even the fact that Mary uses the name that she was accustomed to use with Jesus, "Teacher," suggests verisimilitude, because the Evangelist must have been tempted to have her address Jesus with a more divine appellation. I love this single-verse "Turn," and its eloquent yet earthy six syllables—"Ma-ri-am!"; "Rabb-ou-ni!" Christians believe that some such meeting actually took place between the earliest disciples and the historical, Risen Jesus. This earthy depiction honors that event in a dramatically memorable way.

John chapter 21, often called "The Epilogue" because it seems to have been added *after* the clear conclusion of the original Gospel (in 20:30-31), I call, a little clumsily but I think necessarily, "Jesus' Revelation Means-of-Grace Sermons." Chapter 20 taught us, historically and dramatically, how the Risen Lord met his *first* followers. But the question has to arise: How will He meet all *future* disciples? And I think chapter 21 was written to answer this question through three stories: The Risen Lord will meet all future disciples (1) By Christocentric Proclamation, where—when the Risen Lord has addressed his disciples at the lake with his Word (*"Young men, didn't you catch anything?"*), they respond *three times* with the memorable and Christ-pointing words, *"ho Kurios estin!," "It's the Lord!"* This teaches us that the Risen Lord will *continue* to reveal Himself to his Church *by His Word*, by means of which his faithful disciples, then, will point others to him and say, *"It's the Lord!"* Wherever in Church History believers have faithfully (and excitedly!) pointed to their Addressing Lord, Resurrection Revelation continues to occur.

This text is particularly encouraging to preachers and teachers of the Word.

(2) The second means of grace, taught in the second story in the chapter, is Jesus' warm challenge to Peter (and to every future disciple), who *loves* the Lord (Peter affirms this three times!): *"Feed (Shepherd) My Sheep!"* Here disciples are taught that nourishing, "shepherding," taking good care of those who are evangelized by Christocentric proclamation, is the second major means of grace and revelation. (1) Preach Christ enthusiastically—Point to Him! (2) Take real good care of those who are "caught"—nourish, direct, attend them. (And notice, definitely, *whose* sheep they are, repeated three times for emphasis.)

(3) Peter is, of course, thrilled to be honored by this directive from Jesus. And the final word that Jesus speaks to Peter in this great second paragraph, is *"Follow Me!"* Peter then turns around and whom does he now see? *The Beloved Disciple*, already "Following Jesus"! Aaargh! Peter's Bête Noire! So Peter comes back to Jesus and asks him, *"What about this guy?!"* (v. 21). And Jesus replies, in his last recorded words in the entire Gospel, *"If I want him to stick around until I come back again, what business of yours is that? You follow me!"* (v. 22). The first sentence to Peter here is repeated one more time in verse 23. I think it presents the readers with the third great Means of Grace, by which the Risen

Lord will continue to reveal himself to hearers: the "sticking around Beloved Disciple."

Has the Beloved Disciple "been sticking around" until Jesus returns? What is the Fourth Gospel? I think the third Means of Grace is Written Scripture. The Beloved Disciple has, "stuck around" for and with Jesus' Church in this (now) canonical book. *Littera scripta manet.* "*The written word lasts.*"

Thus Jesus will *continue* to reveal his Risen Reality to the Church, for the world, by three great Means of Grace: (1) By Enthusiastic Christocentric Proclamation ("*It's the Lord!*"), stressed three times in our chapter's opening paragraph (v. 7 twice; v. 12). (2) By the Shepherding Care-Giving of Jesus' Sheep by his Church's caregivers (stressed three times in our chapter's middle paragraph, vv. 15, 16, and 17). And (3) by Written Scripture, like the Beloved Disciple's present Fourth Gospel ("*What if I want him to stick around until I come back again?*)," repeated twice toward the end of the chapter, vv. 22 and 23, and see the dramatic next-to-last verse in the Gospel: "*This [sticking-around] disciple is the one who is bearing witness to these events and who has written these things down, and we [penmen of this Gospel] know that his testimony is true.*"

Every Christian is a deep debtor to those who have enthusiastically pointed him or her to Jesus Christ; and to those who, in faithful and loving obedience to Jesus Christ, have really cared for him or her; and to those like the Beloved Disciple, who, in our present canonical New Testament, have written faithfully about Jesus Christ. Tonight we want to say, in special particular: "Thank you, Risen Lord, for The Gospel According to John." Without it and the other Canonical Writings, we would know practically nothing about you and your world-historical, transforming Truth. Amen.

* * *

Appendices:

I.   Life Experiences in the Gospel of John (In Outline)

II. The Lord's Prayer of Matthew 6, "The Lord's" Lord's Prayer of John 17, & The Children's Catechism Lord's Prayer

III. John's Gospel by Chapters

IV. John in Pictures

APPENDIX I

Life Experiences In The Gospel Of John (In Outline)

1A. THE PROLOGUE: Meaning of "the Word": Lady @ FPC New Haven, CT.

Heroes in Westerns from outside town. "The solution [to] the riddle of life in space & time lies outside space & time" (L. Wittgenstein, *Tractatus Logico-Philosophicus*, 1922, 6.4312). 1:18: Trafalgar Square; Capt. Jack; Jn. Donne, Ballad 15 (#2); Jay Leno; Kenneth Cragg. "One Solitary Life."

1B. THE BAPTIST'S IDENTITY INAUGURAL (3 "I Am Not's"; 3 "I Am's"): Marine; v. 29: *"Look! THE Lamb of THE God, taking away THE sin of THE kosmos!"* (4 emphatic definite articles).

1C. THE 5 "FINDINGS" OF 1:41-46: Hidden Author (vv.40-41)?; Greg Graybill.

2. JESUS' WINE & WHIP SERMONS: HOW JESUS COMES WITH GRACE & TRUTH.

3. A SYSTEMATIC THEOLOGY OF HUMAN SALVATION: *AnthrOpos* 3x, *Pneuma* 5x, *Huios* 5x, *Theos* 3x, *Krisis/KrinO* 4x. Karl Barth's "The Church's . . . Baptism."

4A. JESUS' EXHAUSTION: Jerry Falwell & F. Forrester Church, *Life*, Dec. '94, p. 8.

4B. THE FREE GIFT OF THE H.S. vs. HIGHER-LIFE TEACHING, 4:10 (*DOrean*). The Trinitarian Worship of vv. 23-24, & The Trinitarian Mission of the "*Others*" in v. 38.

5. JESUS' DIVINITY SERMON: How Jesus is Divine— Objectively & Subjectively.

6. THE JOHANNINE *SOLA-FIDE* DISTINCTIVE, vv. 28f. No adjectives or adverbs.

7-8. JESUS' CONFRONTATION SERMONS. See Relief in 7:37-39 & 8:31-32.

9. THE MAN WHO ALWAYS TOLD THE TRUTH. Rousseau, Durant, The Miner.

10. JESUS SEEKS A CHRISTOCENTRIC CHURCH. Barmen (1934) Thesis 1 (#39).

11. JESUS CONQUERS DEATH. (## 4,6,17,18); Muggeridge, Chesterton, 2 Lights.

12. JESUS' VALEDICTORY SERMONS OF TRANSPARENCY.

13. THE BELOVED DISCIPLE IN THE BOSOM OF JESUS = BD:JC::JC:GF (1:18). Forgiveness; Following; Failure (v. 23 = 1st of 7 appearances of BD; 5 with Peter).

14. *"I AM THE WAY, THE TRUTH, & THE LIFE. NO ONE COMES TO THE FATHER EXCEPT BY ME"* (v. 6). Holden Vlg.; LA Times; C.S. Lewis' *Silver Chair.* (RSVP)

15. JESUS' DEEP HOMING PROMISES TO DISCIPLES (cf. 8:31-32). Gospel House: J:Mt, F:Mk, M:Lk, A:Jn, M:Ac, J:Rm, J:Cr, A:GEPC, S:TP, O:HJ, N:PJ, D:Rv.

16. THE CHRISTOCENTRICITY OF THE HOLY SPIRIT, vv. 7-15. Eph. 1:3; Col. 2:9.

17. THE LORD'S PRAYER (LP), THE LORD'S "LORD'S PRAYER" (LLP), & THE CHILDREN'S CATECHISM LORD'S PRAYER (CCLP). *The Joint Declaration on the Doctrine of Justification* (Lutheran World Fed. & Roman Catholic Church, 1999).

18. JESUS' MULTIPLE *"EGO EIMI,"* & PETER'S MULTIPLE *"OUK EIMI."* PILATE'S Q. *"What Is Truth?"*

19. *"Jesus said 'Finished,' bowed his head, & gave over the Spirit'"* (Homer/Bach)

20. HOW THE RISEN LORD REVEALED HIMSELF TO HIS FIRST DISCIPLES: The Race, The Turn, The Mission (Munz/Bunz), The Doubter (Shillito), & The Sum.

21. THE EPILOGUE: JESUS' REVELATION-MEANS-OF-GRACE SERMONS: HOW THE RISEN LORD WILL *CONTINUE* TO REVEAL HIMSELF TO US. (1) By Christocentric Sermon (& Sacrament); (2) By XC Shepherding; & (3) By XC Scripture (= e.g., "The Disciple Who Is Staying Around Until I Come Again") (*Littera scripta manet*). F. Lehman's "The Love of God," vv. 1 & 3 (#26).

APPENDIX II

The LP (Matthew 6)	The LLP (John 17)	The CCLP
LP-0: "Our Father, who art in heaven,"	Jesus lifted his eyes to heaven & said, "Father ..." (v. 1a)	"Our Father, who is in all the skies:"
LP-1: "Hallowed be thy Name."	"Glorify your Son so that the Son may glorify you." (vv. 1 & 5)	"Please show us how wonderful you are!"
LP-2: "Thy Kingdom come."	"Holy Father, keep my disciples in your Name you gave to me ..." (v. 11)	"Please come down & be our King!"
LP-3: "Thy will be done,"	"Keep them from the evil one" (v. 15b)	"Please do whatever you you want to do!"
LP-MCC: "On earth as it is in heaven."	"I am not asking you to take them out of the world ..." (v. 15b)	"Everywhere!"
LP-4: "Give us this day our daily bread ..."	"Sanctify them in the Truth; your Word is is the Truth." (v. 17)	"Please give everybody the food they need!"
LP-5: "And forgive us our debts as we forgive our debtors."	"May they all be one, ... as we are one, ... that the world may believe that you sent me" (vv. 20-23).	"Please forgive us the bad stuff we've done; we're trying to forgive people their bad stuff!"
LP-6: "And lead us not into temptation, but deliver us from evil."	"Father, please, may my believers be with me where I am ..." (v. 24).	"And please keep us from wanting to do more bad Stuff; yes, save us from the devil! In Jesus' Name we pray. Amen."

***

APPENDIX III

John's Gospel By Chapters

I. JESUS' PUBLIC MINISTRY (CHAPS. 1-12)

1: John the Evangelist's & John the Baptist's Jesus Sermons: How Jesus Came

2: Jesus' Wine & Whip Sermons: How Jesus Comes with Grace & Truth

3: Jesus' Nicodemus Sermon: How Jesus Evangelizes, I

4: Jesus' Samaritan-Woman Sermon: How Jesus Evangelizes, II

5: Jesus' Divinity Sermon: How the Son is Related to & Attested by the Father

6: Jesus' Bread Sermon: How Jesus Comes to Us & Wants Us to Come to Him

7: Jesus' Confrontation Sermons, I: How Jesus Defends His Person

8: Jesus' Confrontation Sermons, II: How Jesus Defines His Person

9: Jesus' & the Blind Man's Sermons: The Man Who Always Tells the Truth

10: Jesus' Good Shepherd Sermon: How Jesus Seeks a Christocentric Church

11: Jesus' Lazarus Sermon: How Jesus Conquers Death

12: Jesus' Valedictory Sermons: How Jesus Epitomizes His Public Ministry

II. JESUS' DISCIPLESHIP SERMONS & PRAYER (CHAPS. 13-17)

13: Jesus' Footwashing Sermon: How Disciples Learn Their Identity for Mission

14: Jesus' Father Sermon: How Jesus Brings God the Father for Mission (RSVP)

15: Jesus' Son Sermon: How Disciples Learn Their Home for Mission

16: Jesus' Spirit Sermon (The Paraclete): How Disciples Are Gifted for Mission

17: Jesus' Church Prayer: How Jesus Prays & Disciples Learn to Pray for Mission

III. JESUS' PASSION, RESURRECTION, & ONGOING REVELATION (CHAPS 18-21)

18: Jesus' Court Sermons: How Jesus Rules at His Trials

19: Jesus' Cross Sermons: How Jesus Reigns from His Tree

20: Jesus' Resurrection-Mission Sermons: How the Risen Lord Met His Disciples

21: Jesus' Revelation Means-of-Grace Sermons: How He Continues to Meet Us

*   *   *

APPENDIX IV

John in Pictures

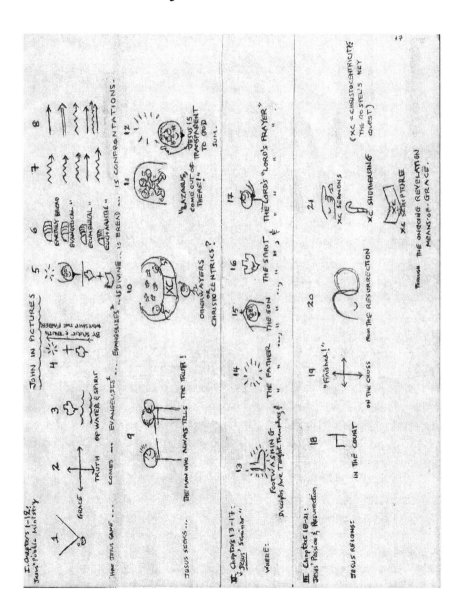

"RELIGIOUS" MANIFESTATIONS IN A MODERNIZING CHINA
What About the West, particularly the United States?

Franklin J. Woo, Monte Vista Grove Homes,
Musings, January 28, 2013

Dear Friends:

I am most grateful for this opportunity to explore with you this evening on how faith (or religion) meets culture in the 21st century. My wife Jean and I have been residents of Monte Vista Grove for 16 years. We are members of Pasadena Presbyterian, a church that intentionally tries to be an inclusive body of Christ in a multicultural society, nation, and world. Before I begin, I have to explain some Chinese ideograms that are pertinent to my talk. Also to understand a culture, one needs to know something about its language and idioms. These are: *zong jiao,* the Chinese rendering of "religion," a term from the Latin *religio,* which did not exist in China, having to borrow it from the Japanese translation, which literally means "religion of the ancestors. *Zhong guo, the* "middle kingdom," is more than a geographic term, meaning for Chinese, the "cultural center of the universe;" as a central national myth that Chinese culture is the perfected wisdom of the world. *Wen,* is a term for literature, or humanities, which I will use for diplomacy, soft power, and "earth community," which I will explain later; and lastly, *wu,* meaning "military," which I will use for power, modernization, and "empire," which also will be explained later.

(All Chinese ideograms have been removed from the manuscript because the publisher does not have the capability to print such.)

I. "RELIGION" SEEN AS COMPLEX, PLURAL, AND PROBLEMATIC

Introduction by a brief recapitulation of the last three Monte Vista Grove Musings, and how they relate to my presentation this evening

1. The last musing by Dale Bruner last year was missed by many of us who were on the first week of our 18-day MVG China travel study. On October 16, 2012 our China travelers were actually walking through Beijing's Tiananmen Square headed in the cold rain towards the Forbidden City. Here at MVG, Dale Bruner has been very gracious in occasionally getting books for me from the Fuller Seminary Library, where he goes daily on foot with his backpack of books, notes, and bottled water. I have often consulted with him regarding the meaning of the New Testament in its original Greek, such as, God so loved the *kosmos*, for the English "world." The Bruner cat, Pumpkin, and our Dr. Jekyll seem to have reciprocity in going into each other's home through their respective cat holes to share food or catnip. The togetherness of Pumpkin and Jekyll is a good metaphor for us. That is, here in this caring and forbearing MVG community, despite our diversity in a broad theological and political spectrum, like the Bruners and ourselves, we are all bound together by common "catechism."

2. A year ago on January 31ˢᵗ was our very first musing with Gary Demarest, who inaugurated the series. He told about how his mind has been changed through interaction with people, largely with those whose views were very different from his. After his presentation on the need to preserve the "peace, unity, and purity" of the church, I sent Gary a memo thanking him for his candid remarks, especially his honesty and transparency. I also said that at one time in the early part of the 20ᵗʰ century, our church had another item besides those of peace, unity, and purity. It was "progress," which was so ambiguous that it was finally dropped. I suggested to Gary that perhaps, just as progress was dropped, so should "purity" be dropped, because no religion is ever really "pure."

Every religion owes much to others, borrowing insights from one another, but often do not give credit. Also, purity can be the occasion for an undesirable "purer than thou" syndrome among and between Christians. Many current-day homophobic people in the church regard homosexuals as impure and even sinful. Gary acknowledged with thanks my memo, but added the words "I am too old to engage in church politics."

3. The second musing was on May 15th by Jane Atkins, who gave a brilliant historical and systematic presentation on the Hispanic ministry of the church. Ricardo Mareno, our new Hispanic pastor at Pasadena Presbyterian claims Prof. Atkins as one of his significant mentors. During the discussion following Jane's talk, Andrew Gutierrez, a recipient of the altruism of Christian mission educators told about his experience at the Presbyterian Allison-James School in Santa Fe, New Mexico. He mentioned its deculturalization process of Mexican American youths who were prohibited to speak Spanish. Andy's poignant recall brought to mind my own experience of the altruism of many Christian missions in San Francisco Chinatown of my youth. Within that small enclave of twenty-four square blocks with a population of 13,000 in the 1930s, were no less than fifteen (15) different brands of Christian missions: Besides the American Baptist, there was an Independent Baptist church. The same can be said about the Presbyterian Church, U.S.A. where less than two and a half blocks away, was the Cumberland Presbyterian Church. Added to these four were a Congregational, a Methodist, an Episcopal called True Sunshine Mission, and also a Roman Catholic St. Mary's Church and its older Cathedral on Grant Avenue, not to mention the YMCA and YWCA and also the Salvation Army for good measure.

I often wondered to myself, are the problems we faced in Chinatown as a minority people in America really denominational? These missions were interested in converting Chinese in hopes that through us will be the eventual conversion of China. Although all these missions in Chinatown antedated the interdenominational Home Missions

Council of North America (1903-1951), they shared one of its chief aims "to rid America of its pockets of foreignism." Listen to what was said in the Minutes of the General Assembly of the Presbyterian Church in 1876 regarding the fear of the influx of Chinese, especially on the Pacific Coast. The G.A. asked that "mission work among them be prosecuted with unceasing vigor, so that their coming among us may not occasion harm to American society, morals, and civil institutions, and that their conversion, by the blessing of God, to the Christian faith may be followed by their consecration to the work of evangelizing their native land." (Robert T. Handy, *A Christian America: Protestant Hopes and Historical Realities.* (Oxford University Press, 1971, p. 75). Here, we can see how 136 years ago, our Presbyterian Church sets itself the task of protecting Protestant America. We can say that this is a clear case of religion protecting culture, an important notion in my talk with you tonight.

With regard to the theme of faith or religion meeting culture in the 21ˢᵗ century, many of us undoubtedly will bring to mind the book by H. Richard Niebuhr entitled Christ and Culture, *published more than sixty years ago by Harper and Row in 1951, being Niebuhr's lectures given at the Presbyterian Austin Theological Seminary in Texas. The book today is a classic. We can recall that Niebuhr speaks about Christ against, of, above, with culture as paradox, and Christ transforming culture. At least, Niebuhr did not speak of Christ destroying or supplanting culture. In the Chinese tradition without a concept of "religion," I tend to speak of religion and culture as synonymous.*

A. "Religion" in Ancient and Modern China was and is its Culture

The religion of China was its great culture, protected by emperors, the ultimate patriarchs and parents of the people and all in the Middle Kingdom. Unlike in Western countries where religion is a separate entity or a dimension of society, the culture of China is the all-encompassing totalistic phenomenon of the entire Chinese social order. That culture includes Nature represented by Daoism, and metaphysics extending to the cosmos, aided by Buddhism which came to China in the first century, CE. To the Chinese their culture is sacrosanct because of its proven ability to sustain a people as a Way of Life for thousands of years. Therefore, we can say that the "religion" (if we are to use this word at all regarding China) is its culture. Throughout the different dynasties of China, the emperors were the guardians and protectors of the culture of the people.

When Buddhism arrived in China from India, it had to be approved by the Board of Sacrifice to show that this foreign religion was no threat to the Chinese way of life. Not only was Buddhism not a threat, it was even an asset, becoming an inherent part of Chinese culture, along with Confucianism and native Daoism. It was in the long process of mutual interaction of several hundred of years that Buddhism was thoroughly sinicized, becoming an inherent part of Chinese ways. For example, an essentially male Indian bodhisattva was in China conveniently transformed into a female intercessor because of her primary role in listening to the problems of women. Chinese Buddhism became known as *chan*. Chan Buddhism went to Korea and from Korea to Japan, where it was called *Zen*, which became popular in many countries of the Western world.

Nestorian Christianity came to China through the silk routes from Persia through Central Asia in the year 635 CE. Tai Zong (627-649), the Tang emperor personally constituted himself as a Board of Rites by issuing a lengthy and favorable description of the Nestorian traders and their religion. He told about their sacred books, prayers, and even the concept of the trinity, using Buddhist language and idioms, the only available terms in saying that the Nestorians were good people, who were no threat to Chinese ways. They were allowed to carry on with their commerce and practice of religion. By the Yuan dynasty under Mongol rule (1260-1368 CE), however, Nestorian Christianity had pretty much disappeared from or absorbed into the Chinese scene. Nevertheless, we can see that Emperor Tai Zong's pronouncement was a virtual "edict of toleration" of a foreign religion.

The 16th and 17th century Jesuits, besides attempting to evangelize ordinary Chinese, were wise to gain not only the approval of the local gentry, but they engaged the Imperial Court as well. They knew that they needed the approval of the highest authority of the land in order to remain in China on a long term basis. With their religion, they also brought to China their mathematics, science (especially astronomy) and gadgetry such as clock-making. They taught cartography in mapping China within the context of the larger world, and even engaged in the manufacturing of cannons for China's military. One recent China scholar refers to the Jesuits as the first European arms dealers. Matteo Ricci (1552-1610) was one of the more prominent Jesuits because of his knowledge of Confucianism, from which he wrote many articles, introducing what he regarded as the great culture of China to the people of Europe. The Jesuits had staffed the Bureau of Astronomy for several hundred years. Their methods of accommodating the gospel of Christ to Chinese culture was greatly challenged by other Catholic orders, leading to Rome curtailing their presence in China for a period. In the mid-1980s, however, Pope John Paul II declared the accommodation method of the Society of Jesus to be correct and can be a model for dialogue with other people of faith.

B. Major Change came in the 19th century and following

By the 19th century things began to change for the Middle Kingdom. Fortified with the freedom of the 16th century Reformation, the rationality of the 17th century Enlightenment, and the power of the late 18th century Industrial Revolution, Britain in the First Opium War (1839-1842) blasted its way into a recalcitrant and self-satisfied, prideful China, and carved out Hong Kong as a British crown colony. Having aped the West in industrialization and military science, Japan in 1895 was able to defeat China in a naval battle over who will rule Korea. Japan gained Taiwan as a Japanese colony, which lasted until 1945 after Japan's defeat in World War II. After a century of such humiliations including those by other foreign powers, China's great culture was no longer seen by Chinese themselves as the center of civilization, the *zhong guo*). Instead of being the epitome of wisdom, Confucian Chinese culture was now blamed as the impediment to progress. Thus began China's tortuous path towards "enriching the nation, and strengthening its military" (*fu guo qiang bing),* by industrializing and modernizing their backward nation. Along with that effort was the concomitant jettisoning of Chinese culture, namely the iconoclastic attacks of Confucianism, which continued throughout the modern period. China scholar Lucian Pye once referred to Modern China as "a civilization pretending to be a nation-state." Nation-state being a Western notion.

C. State Orthodoxy replacing Chinese culture: the existing ruling Party being its protector

A modernizing China began in 1911 with the overthrow of the multi-millennial dynastic rule by Dr. Sun Yat-sen (1866-1925), a medical man, the father of Modern China. By 1927 the rise of the Nationalist Party under the military leadership of Chiang Kai-shek (1887-1975) with Dr. Sun's "Three Principles of the People" (livelihood, power, and democracy) replacing the Confucian system of governance by becoming the state orthodoxy of the newly established Republic of China with the Nationalist Party becoming its guardian. Two decades later, Mao Zedong came to power in 1949 by defeating the Nationalists in a civil war, and Maoist-Marxism became the new state orthodoxy or "religion." Like religion, it demanded total allegiance from the masses of the People's Republic of China. Like the emperors of old, the Communist Party was now the protector and interpreter of state orthodoxy. All other religions are solicited to uphold state orthodoxy on all levels of government: national, provincial, and local.

From this historical perspective, we can see that "religion" as a concept was foreign to China. Religion as an entity was superimposed on China by Protestant Christians whose missionaries arrived in the 19th century and early 20th century.[2] Preoccupied with their anti-Roman Catholic excesses and popery, they were essentially ignorant of Chinese history and culture. They saw and regarded all forms of Chinese religiosities, whether popular or elitist, as pagan and idolatrous. Buddhism and Daoism were seen by them as unscientific superstition. Even Confucianism with its high standards of ethics was to them only an ethics of futility because it depended on human effort alone, without the grace and dependency on almighty God.

Following the pattern set by Nationalist China before 1949, the People's Republic (perhaps reluctantly because of its avowed atheism) also became the arbiter of religion by similarly recognizing five religions as being official: Buddhism, Daoism, Islam, Roman Catholic and Protestant Christianity. All others—the village deities, popular (folk) religions, other Chinese religiosities, urban or rural, vernacular or elitist, were facilely relegated to the category of "feudal superstition." All religions are to come under the regulation by the Bureau of

Religious Affairs (BRA), later becoming known by its new name the "State Administration of Religious Affairs" (SARA).

After the tragic period of the Cultural Revolution (1966-1976), Christians in Western countries were delightfully preoccupied with the resurgence of Christianity in China, and Christianity alone. Some even limited their concerns only to the former Christian missions of their denomination, while the China Christian Council (1980) was trying to inform Western friends that the church in China is "post-denominational." Christians in the West tend not to see the revival of religion as including *all* religions, Buddhism, Daoism, Islam as well as popular religions and folk religiosities. Furthermore, they tend to see the mechanisms of religious regulation of the state council be it BRA or SARA, as essentially control and oppression. In actual practice, the decisions by these state agencies were quite arbitrary and expedient, depending on the workable possibilities in a particular situation. There have been more horse-trading and bargaining than one-sided domination.

Having a dynamism of its own, Christianity in China (both Roman Catholic and Protestant) today has an estimated conservative population from 75-100 million members. Compared to the four million total in 1949, the time of the Communist victory, this is a 19-fold increase, proportionately far exceeding the growth of the entire Chinese population. Christianity in China has to deal with the many mixtures of Christian faith with much of folk beliefs. A well-publicized case, the "Eastern Lightning," our MVG travelers were told, is a contemporary sect that claims that the messiah has come in the form of a woman. With the flourishing of Protestant Christianity in the last few decades, the China Christian Council has established "Theological Construction" as its top priority. This means for the church to recover the values of Chinese culture amid a socialist turned capitalist, rapacious China, through the transforming power of the gospel of Jesus Christ towards a better China and world. The government of the People's Republic has turned its attention in its revisit of Confucian values. Such can be vividly seen in Beijing's spectacular opening ceremony of the summer Olympics in 2008, a global media event where China's cultural contribution to the world was emphasized, including recitations from Confucian texts. Confucian harmony was also the "One World, One Dream" theme of the Olympics. That international event was virtually China's coming-out party, after a century of being at the periphery of the world scene. This new trend of China's place in the world can be seen in the 350 Confucian Institutes established in different parts of the world since 2004.

The large Christian presence in China today may very well be the needed catalyst that will revitalize the Confucian culture in years to come. Wang Zhongxin, a leader of the *Chinese Christian Scholars Association in North America* (Auburndale, MA) draws an analogy from history. Just as interaction between Buddhism (and Daoism) resulted in *songminglixue*, the Neo-Confucianism from the Song dynasty to the twentieth century, likewise interaction between Christian faith and the Confucian culture in the churches and seminaries, with theological construction as a priority, can bring about a revitalization of the latter, which will be relevant to today's China, as well as today's world.[3]

D. A Plethora of Religious Manifestations in a Modernizing China

Well known popular religion in China to the world is the case of the *Falungong, a* religious meditative practice with Buddhist and Daoist insights toward health and wholeness, which arose amid China's rapacious drive in economic reforms and its privatizing of basic medical service beyond the reach of China's majority poor. When unannounced, 10,000 *Falungong* followers appeared as if out of nowhere at the doorsteps of Beijing's *Zhongnanhai,* the headquarters of China's top Communist leaders in April 1999 appealing for their movement to be recognized as an official religion, the paranoid and insecure leaders panicked. In knee-jerk reaction, they declared the *Falungong* not only illegal, but an "evil cult," set to undermine the Communist system. By their reaction Chinese leaders in fact catapulted *Falungong* into international fame with human rights organizations of note in the world claiming it as their *cause célèbre.* Following that incident, all *qigong* (breath-controlled) exercises were banned in China. Today, any form of *qigong* practice, if it exists at all, would play down or eliminate any religious or even philosophical connection to it.

The arbitrary and expedient nature of the PRC decisions on religion can also be seen in their treatment of other folk deities. *Mazu,* the patron saint of seagoing and fishers is a folk religion which originated in China's Fujian province, and it is pervasive in Taiwan today. In the 1980s Taiwanese followers made pilgrimages to their homeland in Fujian carrying with them carefully wrapped images of *Mazu* on their journey. In the PRC *Mazu* has been declared as legal. The traffic of worshippers have been economically beneficial to China and its tourism. On the other hand, *Yiquandao,* a religious sect, the "Connected Path" with Buddhist millenarian background, also originated in China, and is also popular in Taiwan where it is legal. In China it is illegal. Similarly, *Huang daxian,* a religious practice which Hong Kong business people were trying to revive in Guangdong province was met with failure with it being declared as illegal by the Chinese government.

On our Monte Vista Grove trip to China last October 2012, we were guests of an unofficial, but recognized, evangelical church with its charismatic leaders and largely hand-clapping enthusiastic, praise-singing young people. Underground at one time, this church has grown so big that it needed to surface and go public. With its huge sign, "The Caanan Christian Church of Guilin," prominently displayed above its opened entrance, this congregation is today aggressively engaged in outright evangelism. They had properly registered with the authorities for accountability. The church is recognized, but still unofficial.

With regard to being recognized and declared official or unofficial, the same can be said of many of the Chinese non-governmental organizations (NGOs) operating in the PRC. Most of them represent a variety of religious background, although not part of the five officially recognized religions. Yet the government recognizes and encourages their good work of meeting human needs and social uplift. But their religious background, however, is conveniently ignored.

The flourishing of religion and religious organizations in China today within a burgeoning economy and rapidly changing society is dynamic. Religion and all its manifestations are acknowledged to be truly complex and plural, not easily defined or regulated by the old governmental or religious mechanisms for such, either by those of the officially recognized five religions themselves or by the State Administration of Religious Affairs (SARA). China's *zong jiao wen ti,* its "religious question" is a reality, among many other problems facing a modernizing nation in a hurry.

Since China's acceptance into the World Trade Organization (WTO) in 2001, the People's Republic has successfully embraced global capitalism, as if with a vengeance. In our increasingly interdependent world, what similarity (if any), can we see in the West, especially the United States of America, despite great differences between the two cultures, that may be somewhat similar to the phenomenon of religion as being complex and plural, or even problematic? In today's shrinking and globalized interdependent world, the religious question as seen in China today, may very well be not China's alone, so claim an anthropologist and a historian, both with knowledge of sociology and sinology.[4]

In "World Refugee Year" (1960) my wife Jean and I arrived in Hong Kong as staff members of Church World Service (CWS) amid hundreds of thousands of refugees from Communist China.

My task was to direct a job-corps program that enabled hundreds of refugee college students to continue their education while at the same time to spend time in helping thousands of children in the many "rooftop schools," that were set up by churches and voluntary agencies Fresh out of seminary, I thought I knew what religion was all about. But working with Chinese Christians and an assortment of diverse international missionaries in the crowded colony of Hong Kong, I soon began to realize the complexity and plurality of religious faith. Later at the newly established (1963) Chinese University of Hong Kong, more knowledge of Chinese culture was gained from students, and especially from faculty members on an intellectual level. Further study and reading over the years have augmented this unending process of inquiry regarding human hopes and aspirations as seen in religion. Our role as bridge-builders between Christians in the U.S.A. and China had brought us into closer contact, interaction, and we hoped, mutual enrichment with people in China and America. Professionally, I was the director of the China Program of the National Council of Churches in the U.S.A. for seventeen (17) years beginning in 1976 until officially retiring in 1993. With more leisure now, I continue in this quest based on the foundational conviction that God is the Lord of all Creation. This ongoing quest is sustained for me by Christ's continual offer of unmerited grace, which finds no equivalent in Chinese or East Asian traditions where one is supposed to "earn" by human effort alone what one deserves or gains.

II. RELIGION IN THE WEST: NO LESS COMPLEX, PLURAL, AND PROBLEMATIC

A. What About the United States ? An Historical Overview

As an integral part of the European Renaissance which began in the 14th century, the 16th century Reformation resulted in a clash between the "Catholic Substance" of tradition and the "Protestant Principle" of individual rationality and critical thinking. Europe's Thirty Years War (1618-1648) was largely between Roman Catholicism and Protestantism ending with the Peace of Westphalia (1648) with the rise of separate and independent nation states. In short, the rise of nation states in 17th century Europe had relegated religion to a separate sphere of life, namely that of the personal and private. No more do we find a situation of ecclesiastical dominance as in 11th century European Christendom when Pope Gregory VII left King Henry IV, who was in conflict with the magisterium, standing barefooted for three days on the hillside of Canossa.

Although some states embraced a national religion (such as the Church of England, Calvinism in Holland, and Lutheranism among Scandinavian countries), Martin Luther's notion of the "priesthood of all believers" provided the religious foundation for individuality and self-determination. Furthermore, the European Enlightenment of the 18th century with the freedom of science resulted in the rise of paganism, skepticism, and even atheism. These were manifested in the anticlericalism (especially in France) and the attacks on the authority of organized religion, mostly that of Christianity. The devastation of the Thirty Years War resulted in Europe's two hundred year quest for certainty and exactitude. The assumption was that the Newtonian view of Nature could be superimposed on the human realm and society and everything in them could be fitted into precise and manageable rational categories. Great advances were made in every human endeavor, but also with equally devastating unintended consequences.[5] This certainty and exactitude had overwhelming influence on the scholarly methods of inquiry of academia, with the social sciences focusing on only quantifiable data alone lasting throughout the 20th century and beyond.

B. Religion in a "Disenchanted" World

Following the Enlightenment of the 18th century, Max Weber (1864-1920), one of the three giants of sociology along with French Emile Durkheim (1898-1917) and German Jewish Karl Marx (1818-1983), asserted that with the rise of human rationality and the secularization of society, the world is now a "disenchanted" one where magic, miracles and the supernatural no longer dominated. In our time the eminent French philosopher, Marcel Gauchet traced the evolution of religion from animism (spirit in inanimate objects), to polytheism (gods in everything), to monotheism (namely for him Christianity), which he regards as the very "end" of religion. For him, once there is only one God in monotheism, humans are freed from the fears of gods appearing everywhere. That there is a qualitative difference between God of transcendence and earthly mundane life of humans, means that the latter is left on their own, says Gauchet. While God is inscrutable (yet knowable but not totally), humans essentially were left to feign for themselves in this world from which they cannot escape. Nevertheless, it is here on earth that humans need to find meaning and purpose in a disenchanted world, despite the fact of finitude in life and death at the end inevitable. Gauchet ends his trace with atheism.[6]

Meaning and purpose demand that humans need to re-enchant the world amid a secular state and its neutrality towards all religions, particularly in Western countries. In his *Reenchantment of the West,* Christopher Hugh Partridge of England has shown that the process includes a variety of expressions anywhere from alternative spiritualities, sacralization [of secular organizations], popular cultures, and occulture.[7] A Christian attempt to claim that the world has basically never really been disenchanted is by Gordon Graham of Princeton Theological Seminary. As a professor of Theology and Art, he sees Art and aesthetics as a competing alternative to religion.

Lacking in Art communities, claims Graham, is what he terms as ongoing and sustained "festivity." By festivity, I take it that he means the liturgy and regular reenactment of the drama of God's mighty works in history that happens in worship and the celebrations throughout the Christian year. Festivity, in short, has kept the Christian faith viable from generation to generation.[8]

Other examples of diverse manifestations of religion can be seen in the U.S. in the 1960s such as the Hare Krishna people. Many were addicts who found religion to be "the best drug in the world." Others like the Health, Happiness, and Holiness people embracing a crypto Hinduism, or the young in the U.S. turning towards traditions of the East, searching selectively its classical texts, such as the *I-ching,* and the *Taodeching* for edification. Other Asian religiosities followed, such as the Unification Church of the Rev. Sun Myung Moon (1920-2012), founded in South. Korea in 1954 but brought to America in 1971. Unforgettable was Rev. Moon's "blessing" of marriages in one mass event at New York's Madison Square Garden where 2,000 multicultural couples were united in 1982. In our day such religious phenomena as the New Age Religion, Scientology (which purportedly resulted in the high profile divorce of Hollywood celebrity Tom Cruise by wife Katie Holmes), and rock music and its mass concerts have greatly influenced the praise songs in many Protestant and even Roman Catholic churches.

At the Center for Process Studies, Claremont University, CA, based on the open-ended philosophy of organism of British-American philosopher Alfred North Whitehead (1868-1947), which resonates well with Chinese traditions, especially Daoism, are founders John B. Cobb, Jr. and David Ray Griffin, and continued by many others. Griffin's book, *Reenchantment Without Supernaturalism*[9] is another attempt to make sense of a disenchanted world, where religion is a separate, isolated category, where reenchantment is a Constructive Postmodernism effort to put religious values as an ethos of culture. Griffin's eliminating supernaturalism from the picture, however, may not sit well with Christian orthodoxy of either conservatives or liberals. But then, a prominent bishop emeritus of note, John Selby Spong of the Episcopal Diocese of Newark, New Jersey is a strong advocate for doing away with a supernatural spiritual being on whom humans are

71

so dependent to the point of not taking responsibility for their own lives, let alone "wastefully" loving God and neighbor in this world.[10]

In 1998 the Center sponsored an international conference on "Process Thought and the Common Good" in Claremont, CA at which seven participants were from the People's Republic of China. Two of them, Wang Zhihe, an associate of Beijing's Academy of Social Sciences and his spouse Fan Meijun, a professor of aesthetics at the Beijing Normal University ended up being important staff persons of the Center. The Center's China Project that relates to China was established in1994. Through the instrumentality of the new staff, an important "Whitehead in the New Millennium" conference was held in Beijing in 2002. Following that event the Postmodern Development of China was instituted in 2005 for exchanges of scholars between China and Claremont. Since the 2002 conference in less than a decade, close to two dozen universities in China have included process thinking as an emphasis. By 2011, Tang Yijie, professor of philosophy at Peking University cites two intellectual trends in China today as: 1) The zeal for "national essence" or "national character." 2) The other is "Constructive Postmodernism," what the Center for Process Studies has been suggesting to Chinese institutions of higher learning all along.[11]

C. Modernization Undergirded by Protestantism with Unintended Consequences

Max Weber, who was deeply interested in the role of religion in society, saw the attempt to re-enchant the rationalized secular society of modernity as having brought into it the Puritan religious sense of *vocatio* or "calling." This serious intention in the secular context, was sharply analyzed in his *Die protestantische Ethik und der Geist des Kapitalismus,* Weber's greatest work in 1904 in Germany. It was translated into English by Talcott Parsons of Harvard University as *The Protestant Ethic and the Spirit of Capitalism.*[12] Parsons saw in Weber's analysis an optimistic description of human progress in modernity. This optimistic perception was followed by his student, Robert Neely Bellah, who in the mid-1950s was advised by his mentor to look for the Japanese cultural equivalent of the Protestant ethic, under the assumption that modernization will be the panacea for the world's problem of inequality and poverty. Weber's description, however, was no proscription. Contrary to modernity as panacea, Weber was quite pessimistic about the entire process of modernization and so-called human progress, based entirely on rationality, positivistic science and technology. Listen to what he had to say in *Protest nt Ethic and the Spirit of Capitalism:*

"The Puritan wanted to work in a calling; we are forced to do so. For when asceticism was carried out of monastic cells into everyday life, and began to dominate world morality, it did its part in building the tremendous cosmos of the modern economic order. This order is now bound to the technical and economic conditions of *machine production* which today determine the lives of all the individuals who are born into this mechanism, not only those directly concerned with economic acquisition, with irresistible force. Perhaps it will so determine them *until the last ton of fossilized coal is burnt.* In [Bishop] Baxter's view the care for external goods should only lie on the shoulders of the 'saint like a light cloak, which can be thrown aside at any moment.' But fate decreed that the cloak should become *an iron cage.*"[13]

What Parsons (and Bellah) overlooked or ignored was Weber's sense of gloom and doom about the modernization process itself which the latter saw as not only the erosion of time-tested human values, but the strangulation of an *"iron cage,"* which humanity cannot escape *"till the last ounce of fossil-coal is burnt."* Weber's prescience more than a century ago had anticipated our present predicament. If we substitute "fossil fuel" in place of "fossilized coal," Weber's century-old statement speaks loudly to us today. Weber visited America with his wife Marianne, also in 1904. He had strong remarks regarding the United States that "the pursuit of wealth, stripped of its religious and ethical meaning, tends to become associated with purely mundane passions, which often actually give it the character of sport." In the iron cage of modernity we will find, he adds, *"Specialists without spirit, sensualists without heart."* [14] In short, Weber was describing with poignant accuracy, a people whose calling is acquisition, profit, and greed.

What Robert Bellah set out to investigate, he succeeded. He found the cultural equivalent to the Protestant ethic in Japanese Confucianism, and in the process he also discovered a Japanese Confucian scholar,

Ishida Baigan (1685-1744). His work was published in 1957 as *Tokugawa Religion: The Cultural Roots of Modern Japan* (The Free Press) with the conclusion that Japan indeed had the cultural symbolic resources to modernize. Following Japan in the 1970s, the same is to be said of the four mini dragons (S. Korea, Taiwan, Hong Kong, and Singapore), all part of the Confucian civilization which originated in China. Modernization need not be entirely Westernization. Three decades later, however, Bellah reissues his book in 1985 standing firmly on his scholarly research. But in his Introduction (which is well worth the price of the book), he confesses: "I failed to see that the endless accumulation of wealth and power does not lead to the good society but undermines the condition necessary for any viable society at all. I suffered myself from the displacement of ends by means, or the attempt to make means into ends, which is the very source of the pathology of modernization" (p. xviii in *Tokugawa Religion*, 1985). The Confucian culture of Japan which enabled it to modernize, was itself eroded by the modernizing process. In short, modernization destroys cultures and homogenizes them into a common international sameness, albeit with its coveted glitter and gadgetry of convenience of modern living. Many in Modern Japan today in fact feel that they are a hollow people.

A Presbyterian turned Episcopalian, Robert Bellah (1927-2013) claims that he is more a traditionalist who believes that it is still possible to have a grand theory of how the world works and the place of humans in it. After thirty years of being professor of sociology at the University of California, Berkeley, he spends thirteen years in researching and writing *Religion in Human Evolution: From the Paeolithic to the Axial Age,* published by Harvard University Press, 2011. This work of some 746 pages seems to be largely Bellah's own reading notes, with an excellent account of Confucianism. They centered on Karl Jaspers (1883-1969) "axial age," around the first millennium, BCE, where (as if given) the cultural traditions of Greece, Ancient Israel, India, and China, quite independent of one another, all had the symbolic resources for utopian idealism and more importantly, the religious wherewithal for self-criticism and self-correction of their respective status quo. Karen Armstrong, a Roman Catholic, after seven years as a nun, turned scholar of comparative traditions, also made a point of the importance of the axial age in her book, *The Great Transformation: The Beginning of Our Religious Traditions.* (Anchor Books, 2007).

That religion in the United States is also complex and plural can be seen in the book, *Heart and Mind* by Garry Wills of Notre Dame University, a Roman Catholic thinker. Wills sees American Christianity as divided between intellectuals (mind) and ordinary devotees (heart). He describes Christianity in the plural as *Christianities.* Also, Sidney E. Mead (1904-1999) of the University of Chicago and Henry F. May (1915-2012) of the University of California both saw American religion as between that of the Enlightenment and Christian orthodoxy. The tension between these two poles must be kept and not broken; if Christian faith is to be creative.[15] We need to ask, with the plethora of religious expressions in America today, is keeping the two poles in tension for a creative outcome possible?

The prospect for Christianity (both Roman Catholic and Protestant) for the year 2013, according to the prediction by the British magazine, *Economist,* looks grim in losing ground to secularists. Our Presbyterian Church (U.S.A.) with a membership of 2.7 million is reported by *Reuters* as having lost half a million members to date. Recently the issue of sexual orientation has seen West Hollywood Church leaving the Presbyterian fold, because of its conservatism to join the United Church of Christ. Others have or are leaving for precisely the opposite reason, that these perceive the Presbyterian denomination as being too liberal. Some Anglicans have returned to Roman Catholicism. At the same time many people who have nothing to do with organized religion, nevertheless think of themselves as "spiritual" or seeking to be such. Last October, 2012, our Pasadena Presbyterian Church instituted an evening worship in hopes of attracting the hundreds of apartment and condo dwellers in the neighborhood. Its huge sign, prominently displayed in the church patio reads, "Are you spiritually hungry, but institutionally suspicious? Come to our coffee hour and evening service," seems to have captured a public sentiment of our time.

D. Hybridity, Multiple Belonging, and Towards a Dialogical Civilization

Earlier, we mentioned that the 17ᵗʰ century Jesuits in China were wise in accommodating their Christianity to the Chinese Confucian cultural tradition. Equally wise were their Chinese converts who embraced Roman Catholicism (and Western science brought by the Jesuits) *selectively* in accordance to how the faith and new knowledge can enhance their humanity and humane governance of Chinese society. The literati in the Chinese Imperial Court who became Christians were spiritual giants and pillars of Roman Catholicism in China, which lasted to this day. While men like *Paul Xu Guangqi*,1562-1633), *Leo Li Zhizao*,1565-1630), and *Michael Yang Tingyun*,1557-1627) exchanged their Buddhist religion for Roman Catholicism, but as officials in the Chinese bureaucracy, they remained through and through Confucians. They were both truly Roman Catholics and truly Chinese Confucians, a *hybrid* people. Though they adopted new ideas and new values, they did so always on their own terms.[16]

In January 1989, a young Chinese visiting scholar named *Yang Fenggang* [17] arrived in America to collect material for his teaching of Christianity in China. The student protest and subsequent Beijing massacre on June 4, 1989 resulted in him and many other intellectuals not returning to China. Yang pursued a doctoral degree in sociology at the Catholic University in America, while participating in an evangelical Community Christian Church of Greater Washington, D.C., where he was baptized in 1992. His doctoral dissertation was a study of Chinese churches in America, concluding that they were virtual social mechanisms which enabled Chinese immigrants, old and new, to *selectively* assimilate both to American life while also *selectively* retaining their Chinese culture. Yang became professor of sociology and Chinese religion at Indiana's Purdue University. He is recognized as an authority of Chinese religion, both in the U.S.A. and China. In his research in recent years on Christianity in Hong Kong, Taiwan, China, North America and elsewhere in the world, he came to another conclusion: That all Chinese Christians are "Confucian Christians" or "Christian Confucians," depending on which tradition is the core for them.

The same could be said about Korean Christians who come from a cultural background of Neo-Confucianism of more than half a millennium from 1392-1910 in the Yi (Chosen) dynasty.[18] Although most Korean Christians are so grateful to the missionary movement which introduced their country to Christ, few try to relate Christian faith to their Confucian heritage intellectually. An unusual scholar is Heup Young Kim, professor of systematic theology at Korea's Kangnam University who tries to do so with no attempt to "Confucianize Christianity, or Christianize Confucianism." He urges Christians not to displace, but to include their culture as an expression of Christian faith.[19] One of my former colleagues and close friends was Julia Ching,1934-2001),[20] a former Roman Catholic nun of the Ursuline Sisters, who left the convent after two decades and became a scholar of Asian Studies. She taught in Australia, New York's Columbia University, Yale in New Haven, and Canada's University of Toronto. She died at a young age with cancer. Ching considered herself a "Confucian-Christian," a "hyphenated person," bridging two cultures.

Another person of dual belonging is Yeo Khiok-Khng,[21] a Malaysian Chinese who is professor of New Testament at the United Methodist Garrett-Evangelical Seminary, Evanston, Illinois. Yeo says he is *both* a Christian and a Confucian and is trying to understand and teach Christianity from a bicultural perspective. I have a coterie of friends and colleagues (both Anglos and Asians) at the School of Theology, Boston University who refer to themselves as "Boston Confucians." A scholar, Daniel A. Bell, who teaches political philosophy at Beijing's prestigious Tsinghua University and is enamored with Chinese culture, considers himself a "Canadian Confucian."[22] This is not to mention many Anglo Americans who have wholeheartedly embraced Buddhism as their religion, with some even becoming teaching masters of the tradition. Rose Drew, a scholar in Scotland and also Sweden, has done research in interfaith relations. In her doctoral work, she has explored the notion of dual religious belonging. In her study of six prominent scholars who claim dual belonging, she found that though theologically they could not integrate two faiths coherently, they nevertheless were able to live within the theologically unresolved tension. They can put emphasis on one or the other as a helpful spiritual resource, depending on the given situation.[23] One of my mentors (John Cobb) suggested that dual belonging makes sense, if we see two religious traditions as mutually dependent features of the totality of reality. It is like the proverbial elephant being explained by blind persons holding onto only its trunk, leg, or feeling its side.

In our rapid and all too brief survey of faith meeting culture in China and the West, namely the United States of America, we can say that religion and culture are virtually inseparable. Though they are considerably different in both these places, they are nevertheless in both China and the U.S.A. very complex, plural, and even problematic.

The great challenge to all religions, cultures, and all people of goodwill, faith or no faith in China and the United States (the two most powerful nations in today's world) is to rise to the occasion to work collaboratively in bringing the best of their central tradition in encouraging the rest of the world by example, to solve the pressing planetary problems of our time. In an uncomplicated categorization, of the fundamental problem of our time, international activist David C. Korten of the Positive Future Network, Bainbridge Island, Washington, classified it as the tension between "Empire" and "Earth Community." His call is for the world to turn (*metanoia*) from Empire to Earth Community.[24] I have appropriated his simple classification by using two Chinese ideograms, *wu,* for empire, and *wen,* for earth community.

Johann Wolfgang von Goethe's *Faust* worked with the devil in grasping all knowledge to gain power over the world. In the frenetic process, he lost wisdom.

In remorse he tried to regain it, to which was said to him *Erquickung hast du nicht gewonnen, Wenn sie dir nicht aus eigner Seele quillt,* which is to say, "Recovery will not come, unless it is out of your very soul." In our modern disenchanted world of positivistic science, secularity, and its complexity, plurality, and problematic religion and culture, we too need to recover knowledge as wisdom. It also will not come, unless out of the very God-given soul of a people. Furthermore, the plurality of the multicultural world renders no particular religion or culture to remain in isolation, let alone having all the wherewithal to meet today's needs. One way or another every tradition is impacted by the plurality of diverse traditions surrounding it. Its needs to interact and work together with all for the greatest common good.

Following in the spirit of openness of an encyclical of Vatican II, *Pastoral Constitution in the Modern World*, which states that the "joys and hopes, the grief and anguish" of the world are also those of Christian people, the Roman Catholic Church today is taking the lead in relating and interacting with other people of faith, with the conviction that "the holy spirit offers to all the possibility of being made partners in a way known to God, as the paschal mystery" (*Gaudium et Spes*, 1965). A recently published comprehensive 605-page study shows how serious and thorough Catholic scholars have been in understanding traditions other than their own.[25] It is in interacting in dialogue with others that we can come to an even more profound understanding of ourselves. In our time of complexity and plurality, not to mention its manifold problems—to build a dialogical civilization is the imperative towards a peaceful, sustainable, and harmonious planet, where all can live and grow. Thank you for listening to my musing.

NOTES:

2. Mayfair Mei-hui Yang, editor, *Chinese Religiosities: Afflictions of Modernity and State Formation.* (University of California Press, 2008), p. 12 of her Introduction.

3. "A Summary on the *Ru* Tradition and East-West Seminar" by Tan Tianjiao in *Chinese Christian Scholars Association in North America,* No. 57, July to December, 2011, pp. 16-18.

4. Vincent Goossaert and David A. Palmer, *The Religious Question in Modern China.* (University of Chicago Press, 2011).

5. Stephen Toulmin, *Cosmopolis: The Hidden Agenda of Modernity.* (The Free Press, 1990).

6. Marcel Gauchet, *The Disenchantment of the World: A Political History of Religion.* (Princeton University Press, 1999). From animism to polytheism to monotheism to atheism.

7. Christopher Hugh Partridge, *Reenchantment of the West.* (London: T& T Clark, 2000).

8. Gordon Graham, *The Reenchantment of the World: Art and Religion.* (Oxford, 2007).

9. David Ray Griffin, *Reenchantment Without Supernaturalism: A Process Philosophy of Religion.* (Cornell University Press, 2001).

10. John Selby Spong, *A New Christianity for a New World: Why Traditional Faith Is Dying and How Faith Is Being Born.* (HarperSan Francisco, 2001).

11. For an account of how two scholars from the People's Republic of China got involved in the work of the Center for Process Studies, see: Wang Zhihe and Fan Meijun, *Second Enlightenment.* (Beijing: Peking University Press, 2011), and Wang Zhihe, *Process and Pluralism: Chinese Thought on the Harmony of Diversity.* Foreword by Dr. John B. Cobb, Jr.

(Frankfurt, Germany: Ontos/Verlag, 2012). See also "The Enlightenment and Its Difficult Journey in China by Tang Yijie, Translated by Franklin J. Woo in *Process Perspective,* Newsmagazine of the Center for Process Studies, Vol. 34, No. 2, Spring 2012.

12. Max Weber, *The Protestant Ethic and the Spirit of Capitalism.* Translated by Talcott Parsons. With a Foreword by R. H. Tawney. (Charles Scribner's Sons, 1958).

13. Weber, p. 181, emphasis added.

14. Weber, p. 182, emphasis also added.

15. Garry Wills, *Head and Heart: American Christianities.* (Penguin, 2007); Sidney E. Mead, *The Nation with the Soul of a Church.* (Harper & Row, Publishers, 1975); and Henry F. May, *The Divided Heart: Essays on Protestism and the Enlightenment of America.* (Oxford University Press, 1991).

16. Benjamin A. Elman, *On Their Own Terms: Science in China, 1550-1900.* (Harvard University Press, 2005).

17. Yang Fenggang, *Chinese Christians in America: Conversion, Assimilation, and Adhesive Identities.* (The Pennsylvania University Press, 1999) and his *Religion in China: Survival & Revival Under Communist Rule.* (Oxford University Press, 2012).

18. Peter K. Bol, *Neo-Confucian History.* (Harvard University Press, 2008).

19. Heup Young Kim, *Christ and the Tao.* (Christian Conference of Asia, 2003).

20. Julia Ching, *Confucianism and Christianity: A Comparative Study.* (Tokyo: Kodansha International and The Institute for Oriental Religions, Sophia University, 1977).

21. K. K. Yeo, *Musing with Confucius and Paul: Toward A Chinese Christian Theology.* (Eugene, Oregon: Cascade Books, 2008).

22. Daniel A. Bell, *China's New Confucianism: Politics and Everyday Life in a Changing Society,* (Princeton University Press, 2008).

23. Rose Drew, *Buddhist and Christian? An Exploration of Dual Belonging.* (Routledge, 2012).

24. David C. Korten, *The Great Turning: From Empire to Earth Community.* (San Francisco: Berrett-Koehler Publishers, Inc. 2005). (Korten's historical context is 5,000 years of history.)

25. Karl A. Becker and Ilaria Morali (eds.), *Catholic Engagement with World Religions: A Comprehensive Study* with collaboration of Maurice Borrmans & Gavin D'Costa. (Maryknoll, NY: Orbis Books, 2010). (Clear on Christian non-negotiables in interreligious dialogue.)

Appendix A

To illustrate the lecture, Franklin Woo set up a miniature museum to amplify his talk with the following show-and-tell items:

1. Photo of a **Pacific islander in dance** to show that religion in prehistoric and pre-linguistic times began when, amid survival through hunting, fishing, and later, farming, human found time to play. *Homo ludens* (playful humans) expressed their linkage to the holy through *dance, music, song, and rhythm.* These were the primordial experience of religion, passed on orally, way before they were articulated, and systematized in religious texts.

2. Painting of a **Chinese scenery** of mountains, stream, and foliage with a very small human under a gazebo. Chinese *Daoism* sees the universe as an organism.

   As latecomers to earth, humans are a very small (but not insignificant) part of this vast cosmos. As an integral part of the *Dao*, humans need to co-create with it. As the Chinese version of the prologue to the Gospel according to John has it, "In the beginning was the *Dao,* the *Dao w*as with God, and the *Dao* was God."

3. A scroll of **bamboo.** "To bow and to bend, we shan't be ashamed" (Shaker hymn). Learn from the bamboo, knowing that it will always spring back to its original position. Yielding and give way to opposition; winning a war without fighting; this is Chinese and East Asian martial arts. (Sun Tzu, *The Art of War.*)

4. A scroll with **a mountain appearing as a person**, both are indistinguishable. A sage is a prudent person of wisdom and good judgment through much experience and reflection. The Chinese ideogram for sage consist of human, *ren* on the left side and mountain, *shan* on the right side.

5. Calligraphy, *chun fu*, "**Spring blessing**" is a symbol of hope. In the rhythm of the passing seasons, Spring has a resurrectional quality when new tender leaves begin to appear on bare

Winter branches. From the lunar calendar, Chinese New Year in 2013 came on February 10th. At the time, part of the 200 million "floating population" of rural workers to China's urban expansion was heading home to celebrate this sacred "Spring Festival" with their families, seeing them on this rare once-a-year event. Spring is a time of new beginning. The Chinese term for the Gospel of God in Jesus Christ is *fu yin,* "The sound of Blessing." (calligraphy by Atina Young, age 6.)

6. Booklet, *tong shu,* is a **Chinese almanac**, comparable, but much more comprehensive than a Farmer's Almanac. It offers practical advice on auspicious days to wed, to begin a business, or to travel, or not to do so. It covers a variety of daily concerns from first-aid to pre-natal care to proper ethical behavior. The red string attached to the booklet means that this valuable volume should be hung at an easily accessible place, such as near the kitchen. An updated version for each year can be purchased in any supermarket in China, or even here in San Gabriel Valley. *Tong Shu* is part of Chinese culture.

7. Buddhism came to China from India in the first century CE. Over the centuries it became sinicized, an integral part of Chinese culture.

   Intellectually, Chinese *chan* Buddhism went to Korea, then to Japan where it is known as *Zen.* Three concrete examples of sinicized Buddhism on the level of popular religion:

   a. The ***Maitreya Buddha*** of the future (happy Buddha) in the Chinese ethos of family and ancestor veneration, are seen here surrounded by five grandchildren. (Celibacy in Buddhism?)

   b. ***Guan Yin***, the goddess of Mercy, is one who listens to all the sighs and beckoning of women, especially their desire for children. The original Indic bodhisattva was more a male figure. Chinese felt that it would be inappropriate to have a man listening on problems of women. Chinese pragmatism won out.

Two very unorthodox "vegetarian" **Buddhist monks statuettes**, who not only enjoy eating meat, but also seen here in a state of satisfied stupor after emptying their wine bowls.

8. A **Nestorian cross**. The cross on the rubbing from the limestone monument is so small, that it is difficult to see. Here you can clearly see the three little circles at the four ends of the cross, representing the Trinity.

   Alongside of the cross are stylized clouds, symbolizing Daoism, and underneath the cross is a huge lotus flower, the symbol of Buddhism.

   One interpretation of this arrangement is that Christianity is the fulfillment of the aspirations of Chinese tradition as represented by Daoism and Buddhism. From today's perspective, this may appear to be chauvinistic with a sense of Western superiority, although Nestorianism was actually part of the Church of the East

9. *Jing*, the Chinese (and East Asian) ideogram for "**respect**," the very basic attitude and posture, as the fundamental starting point, for all relationships, whether in the social or natural environment. Relating to all humans, sentient beings, and objects in all of God's creation with *jing, r*espect, all principles can be fathomed, and all mystery entered into.

   Mutual respect is the *sine qua non* in interfaith and intercultural dialogue.

10. A miniature couplet of *Xian tian xia zhi you er you; Hou tian xia zhi le er le. i*s a replica of two scrolls, which have been hanging in Marwick Place for more than a decade and a half. The couplet is known as "a scholar's declaration" to be "the first under heaven to worry about the problems [of the world]," and "the last under heaven to enjoy its benefits." The scrolls were given as a gift to Monte Vista Grove by the travel study group to China in 1998, after they hung the couplet in Marwick as part of their trip report.

Appendix B

Before his lecture, the presence of invited guests was acknowledged and introduced by the speaker:

The Rev. Drs. Dickson Yagi and Paul Nagano and spouse Florence of the Council for Pacific Asian Theology (CPAT).

The Rev. Hugh Wire and Dr. Anne Wire, professor of New Testament (emeritus) of San Francisco Theological Seminary. The Wires have been on several occasions teachers at the Nanjing Union Theological Seminary, China through the Amity Foundation.

Ms. Yan Ronghui and Ms. Yang Liantao,two theological teachers from the Zhejiang Theological Seminary, China, on their six-month study of pastoral counseling at Fuller Theological Seminary.

The Rev. Dr. Peter and Mrs. Lai, formerly pastor of the True Light and the First Presbyterian Church in Alhambra. In retirement Dr. Lai has been working with university students from China studying in southern California.

Drs. Fan Meijun and Wang Zhihe of the China Project and Postmodern Development of China, Center for Process Studies, Claremont University. (They were announced as probably being late, but actually they did not arrive.)

Dr. Donald and Mrs Mei Ling Ouyang, and Thea Van Amersfoort who were members of the Monte Vista Grove October 2012 travel study trip. The group included executive director Debbie Herbert and spouse Bill, as well as residents Mas Hibino and Hannah Kang.

Friends from Westminster Gardens of whom only Andrew Gutierrez was mentioned, since he was to be referred to in the lecture.

Also present was Robert Martin (retired educator) of the Okinawa Association of America.

# # # # #

WHERE MUSLIMS AND CHRISTIANS MEET: POLITICAL AND MISSIONAL ISSUES

J. Dudley Woodberry. Monte Vista Grove Homes, Musings, June 27, 2012

The flag of the Egyptian Independence Movement in 1919 displayed a cross within a crescent, symbolizing Egyptian Muslims and Christians together expressing their joint opposition to their foreign colonial masters. This same symbol was displayed in the heady days of the Arab Spring to express again their joint opposition, this time to indigenous autocratic rule. The symbol was meant to convey harmony between Muslims and Christian, but at times the crescent seemed to Christians more like jaws clamping down on them, and the cross to Muslims seemed more like a fishbone stuck in their throats. In both its positive and negative connotations it reflects the three questions we shall consider all too briefly here. In Muslim politics, what is the likelihood of peace? And, what is the likelihood of freedom of religion? And in this context, how are Muslims following Christ?

In Muslim Politics, What is the Likelihood of Peace?

My wife, Roberta, and I experienced the contrast between the militancy and peace of Muslims on 9/11/2001 when we were in Peshawar and one year later on 9/11/2002 when we were returning to Peshawar. On the earlier date we were gathering for a farewell party for a pilot who was leaving PACTEC, an aviation and communication program that our son had been directing in Afghanistan from Peshawar. A pilot came in and informed us that BBC had reported that a plane had flown into the World Trade Center. We checked on our computers and saw a miniature picture with flames the size of a burning match, but which ignited years of conflict. With flight permission for PACTEC cancelled by both the Taliban in Afghanistan and Pakistan's Inter-Services Intelligence and the expulsion of all known Christian workers from Afghanistan, we returned to the U.S. while our Muslim neighbors and strangers alike expressed their sorrow.

One year later to the day we were returning to Peshawar and from there to Kabul. Well before sunrise we were flying down the western coastline of Iran—which had produced both the Khomeini revolution and the 15ᵗʰ Century Muslim Sufi poet Jami, who wrote, "Seek healing from the Christ for he from this and every fault will set you free." On the plane before dawn pious Muslims did their ablutions in the lavatories and prayed the same ritual prayers for protection that the terrorists had prayed a year earlier before killing hundreds.

Between planes in Dubai we visited the mud palace where the governing sheik had in previous years served thousands of cups of coffee in hospitality rather than hostility. Then we toured the mud madrasa next door, where children were taught rabbinic type values rather than the hate taught in the Taliban (lit. students) madrasas of Pakistan. Back on another plane from Dubai to Peshawar my elderly seatmate rocked back and forth the entire flight chanting quranic verses for protection— many of them quoted by the highjackers a year earlier. As we landed in Peshawar the calls to evening prayer echoed throughout the city—some from militant mosques, some from peaceful.

The dual peaceful and militant messages can be traced back to the life of Muhammad, where his words and actions are more peaceful in his early life in Mecca, where he represented a persecuted minority, than in his later life in Medina, where he turned to political and military expansion as a means of building an earthly kingdom of God. Thus the order is the reverse of the Bible where the military expansion is in the Old Testament and the message of loving our enemies is more in the New. We see the contrasting perspectives within the Quran. On the one hand, in a passage referring to Jews, Christians, and Muslims, it says, "We [God] have assigned a path to each of you. If God had so willed, he would have made you one community, but he wanted to test you, so compete with each other to do good" (5:48). On the other hand, it says, "Fight in the way of God those who fight you . . . . Kill them . . . . Fight them until there is no more persecution and faith is in God" (2:190-193). And it commands, "Fight and slay the infidels" (9:5).

In history there have been both military jihads, as in the early expansion of Islam in the Middle East, and peaceful trade accompanied by Sufi mystics and legal qadis as in much of the expansion in Southeast Asia. Both patterns are seen in Sunni and Shiite Islam. For example, the Sunni Hanafi Deobandis have been peaceful in India but were the source of the Taliban in Pakistan. And the Shiite Imam Komeini was more militant, while a former Iranian president Khatami and the current president Rouhani are more peaceful.

Recent events have included bombings from September 11, 2001 to the Boston Marathon on April 15, 2013. But there have also been peaceful elections of moderates like Rouhani and Islamists like the Hamas in Gaza, Hizbollah in Lebanon, and the Muslim Brotherhood supported candidates in Egypt. Yet what started as the relatively peaceful demonstrations of the Arab Spring have morphed into deadly clashes in Egypt, Syria and beyond.

Although Muslims tend to view Islam as permeating all of life, other factors than "religion," narrowly conceived, affect the turmoil in the Muslim World. One is group solidarity (Arabic 'asabiya) based on ethnicity, tribe, religion, sect, etc., and those who are included in the group are commonly determined by the perceived enemy—be it Israel or Shiites. A second factor is that the national boundaries were commonly drawn by colonial powers and often dissected or otherwise divided ethnic groups like the Pashtuns of Pakistan and Afghanistan or the Kurds of Turkey, Syria, Iraq, and Iran. A third is demographics where, for example, Shiites ranked third after Christians and Sunnis in the census of 1932 in Lebanon when government offices were determined by faith community. However, now Shiites are the majority and Christians (enlarged by many Palestinian refugees) third in size after Sunnis. Finally, there is the interrelated cultural cluster of the felt need for honor, justice, and often revenge—hence the tendency by harmed groups to remember the Crusades, the establishment of modern Israel, the Holocaust, or the Turkish massacre of Christians.

Yet Muslims have been involved in a number of recent overtures for peace and understanding. Some of us at Fuller Seminary were involved in a number of these dialogues besides meeting regularly with Muslim leaders in the Los Angeles area. The Common Word Consultation which met at Yale University and elsewhere focused on areas where Muslims and Christians have much in common and produced a book <u>A Common Word: Muslims and Christians on Loving God and Neighbor.</u>[26] Fuller had a series of consultations with the Salam Institute of Peace and Justice at the American University in Washington, DC. We first agreed that our working on peace would not have any ulterior motives. At the same time we suggested guidelines on sensitive issues such as how to engage in mutual respectful witness. These may be found in <u>Peace-Building By, Between, and Beyond Muslims and Evangelical Christians</u>[27]. Discussions in Turkey explored Muslim and Christian ways of finding peace with God and each other published as <u>Muslim and Christian Reflection on Peace: Divine and Human Dimensions</u>[28], also published in Turkish translation.

Returning to our original question, in Muslim politics, what is the likelihood of peace? It is certainly possible, for there are building blocks for it from the earliest period of Islam to the present. However, currently religious persecution of both non-Muslims and other Muslims of a different sect is high in Muslim countries and religious freedom is low and the two phenomena appear to be linked.[29] In fact Brian Grim and Roger Finke note that "Governments in more than seven in ten Muslim-majority countries harass Muslims compared with Muslims being harassed in only three in ten Christian-majority countries."[30] Therefore, there is not currently likelihood of much peace in Muslim politics, and this leads us to the next question.

---

[26] Eds. Miroslav Volf, Prince Ghazi bin Muhammad, and Melisa Yarrington. Grand Rapids: Eerdmans, 2010.

[27] Eds. M. Abu-Nimer and David Augsburger. Lanham, MD: Lexington Books, 2009, On the guidelines see J.D. Woodberry, "Toward Mutual Respectful Witness", pp. 171-177.

[28] Eds. J.D. Woodberry, Osman Zumrut, and Mustafa Koylu. Lanham, MD: University Press of America, 2005.

[29] Brian J. Grim and Roger Finke, <u>The Price of Freedom Denied: Religious Persecution and Conflict in the Twenty-First Century.</u> New York: Cambridge University Press, 2011. Chap.6

[30] Page 185.

In Muslim Politics, What is the Likelihood of Freedom of Religion?

When we look to Islam's past we get mixed examples. We have noted the quranic passage referring to Jews, Christians, and Muslims, "We [God] have assigned a path to each of you . . . so compete with each other to do good" (5:48). A Meccan passage also says, "The [Muslim] believers, the Jews, the Christians, and the Sabians—all who believe in God and the Last Day and do good—will have their reward with their Lord. There is no fear for them, nor will they grieve" (2:62). Another passage says, "There's no compulsion in religion" (2:256). Also Muhammad granted permission for the Christians of Najran in southwestern Arabia to have freedom of worship as long as they were loyal and paid a tax[31]—an example, we Christians shared with Saudi Arabian officials when they tried to restrict our worship in the 1970's and 80's. However, the Quran does enjoin killing apostates in a context where they join the hostile enemy (4:88-90).

There are also traditions (hadith) ascribed to Muhammad which prescribe the death penalty for apostasy, but they seem to indicate that the apostates joined the enemy.[32] However, the idea of death for apostasy developed more after Muhammad when some tribes that had previously allied themselves with him and the Muslim community broke away. When the first caliph Abu Bakr fought against them, the battles were called the Rida (apostasy) Wars. He viewed apostasy as treason against the developing Muslim state, hence punishable by death. Later Muslims divided the world between the "House of Islam" and the "House of War," though subsequently the "House of Treaty (sulh)" was added. And monotheists like Jews and Christians were given a separate status as dhimmis who were protected but were second class.

In the contemporary period we see a broad spectrum of attitudes toward religious liberty. Many liberals support religious freedom,[33]

---

[31] W. M. Watt, <u>Muhammad at Medina</u>. (Oxford: Clarendon Press, 1956), 359-360.

[32] Eg. al-Bukhari, Sahih al-Bukhari, ed. M.M. Khan. (Beirut: Dar al-Arabiya, 1405-1975, v.9, p.11 [Bk. 83 ch.6 (al-Diyat), trad. 17]).

[33] See C. Kruzman, ed. <u>Liberal Islam</u> (New York: Oxford University Press, 1998), 59-326; A. Sachedina, <u>The Islamic Roots of Democratic Pluralism</u> (New York: Oxford University Press, 2001).

but on the street we often see the opposite. When Roberta and I first went to Afghanistan to pastor the church, an expatriate family was arrested for giving out four Gospels of Luke in the bazar, and we had to give a Muslim lawyer a defense based on quranic verses to get him released. Later the blind Afghan leader of the underground church had his tongue cut out and then was killed by a mujahideen leader so he could not mention the name of Jesus again. European participants in an underground Afghan church were killed in front of their children. The struggle on both sides for the soul of Islam is intense.

The Malaysian Osman bin Bakr, who was at Georgetown University, noted in one of our dialogues that Muslims as they spread kept including more people in the accepted category of "People of the Book"—for example, Hindus and Buddhists in Indonesia. Even the major ideologue of the Muslim Brotherhood, Sayyid Qutb (d. 1966), though he espoused a narrow position that Islam should be accepted by all because it includes the other religions, argued that faith could not be coerced because it would then no longer be faith.

The tensions within the Muslim community also surface on the international level. The International Declaration of Human Rights is in the United Nation's Charter states that freedom of religion is an unqualified right, and all nations must sign it when they join the UN (though a number of Muslim nations have tried to delete it).[34] Some Muslim nations have made alternate declarations: The Universal Declaration of Human Rights (1991) by the Islamic Council of Europe and the Declaration of Human Rights in Islam (1990) by the Organization of Islamic Conference (OIC) in Cairo. Both are somewhat ambiguous and the Arabic and English texts are slightly different. There are three areas of tension:

1. For the UN religion is a matter of personal choice and secularism is implied, while for Islam religion involves human obligations base on God's Law.

---

[34] D. Little, J. Kelsay, and A. Sachedina, <u>Human Rights and the Conflict of Culture: Western and Islamic Perspectives on Religious Liberty</u> (Columbia: University of South Carolina, 1988), 3-12, 101-105.

2. For the UN there is no distinction between people while for Islam there is a distinction between Muslims and non-Muslims and men and women.

3. For the UN there is freedom of thought, conscience, religion and freedom to change religion while in Islam there is traditionally no freedom to change from being a Muslim.[35]

The Law of Apostasy, in slightly different forms affirms that someone who leaves Islam may or should be killed. Maududi (d. 1979), the very influential Indo-Pakistani Islamist revivalist who founded the Jamaat-i-Islami in Pakistan, on at least one occasion affirmed this. Conversely Fazlur Rahman (d. 1988), the Pakistani liberal reformer and educator, argued against this law because he did not find it clearly in the Quran, and support for reports of it in the Traditions (hadith) were weak.

When we return to our question "In Muslim politics, what is the likelihood of freedom of religion?" we see that the answer is related to how various Muslims understand Islamic law. Shariah (lit. a path to the water hole) is used by the conservative Islamist scholars (ulama) to refer to the will of God as expressed in the Quran and the canonical traditions (hadith) of the example (sunna) of Muhammad plus its developments through jurisprudence (fiqh) during the first three centuries of Islam. At that time, in their view, the door to further interpretation (ijtihad) was closed. The Islamist revivalists like the Muslim Brotherhood traditionally restricted their authorities to the Quran and Sunnah but wanted the door for scholarly interpretation (ijtihad) left open for new interpretations. Liberals also want the door to new interpretation open, though some want Shariah just to include Islamic values from the Quran and the practice of Muhammad.

A recent Gallup Poll of Muslims around the world indicated that what Muslims most admire about the West is its technology and democracy, yet when they themselves have exercised this democracy in recent years

---

[35]   A.E. Mayer, Islam and Human Rights, 3rd ed. (Boulder, CO: Westview Press, 1999), 19-24, 52-53, 76-78, 89-94, 149-150.

it has often included some form of Shariah.[36] However, they have no uniform understanding of what that Shariah means.

One problem in trying to mix Western and Islamic systems was evident in Afghanistan in 2006. An Afghan, Abdul Rahman, was sentenced to death for having converted from Islam to Christianity. Article 2 of the constitution says that all citizens "are free to exercise their faith and perform their religious rights within the limits of the provisions of law." But Article 3 says, "no law can be contrary to the beliefs and provision of the sacred religion of Islam." The Afghan government was caught between international demands for Rahman's release and local demands for his execution. The American ambassador asked me to facilitate resolving the case as quietly as possible.

Muslims do not need to choose between an Islamic political/social system and secularism. An alternative example is the Pancasila system in Indonesia that recognized belief in God in a plurality of religions though it limits them to five designated ones.

With these examples in mind, what is the probability in Muslim politics of freedom of religion? Many of the building blocks are there in historical examples and contemporary Muslim thought but, as the encounter in Egypt shows, the road promises to be a long one. This leads Christians to our concluding question.

In this Context, How are Muslims following Christ?

The turmoil between Muslim factions has also impacted Christians. At the beginning of the Arab Spring in Egypt some Egyptians painted the symbol of the cross within the crescent on their cheeks and hands as it had adorned the flags of the 1919 Independence Movement, and Muslims and Christians protected each other in Tahrir Square at times of prayer. However, by the time of this writing dozens of churches and Christian buildings had been burned by supporters of the deposed President Morsi including two Bible Society buildings, the Coptic Church of the Virgin Mary and Anba Abram in Minya province that

---

[36] J.L. Esposito and D. Mogahed. <u>Who Speaks for Islam? What a Billion Muslims Really Think</u> (New York: Gallup Press, 2007), p 36.

had been a place of prayer for 1,600 years. One report stated that Muslims had held Friday prayer in three of the churches so that they would become mosques and could not be used as churches. On one burned building was written in Arabic, perhaps with black from the ashes, "Love your enemies" and "We will not stop praying." And many Muslims have supported the Christians. Yet thousands of Christians in Syria and elsewhere have become refugees. Some Assyrian Christian refugees from Thawrah, Syria, were told by some of the opposition militia, "If you want to come back, convert to Islam, or you will be killed."

Yet an interesting phenomenon has occurred in recent years. Where militant forms of Islam have taken over countries and/or Islamic Law has been imposed, and there has been a friendly Christian presence, there has been receptivity to the Gospel with its message of love and forgiveness. This was noted in Iran after the Khomeini Revolution of 1979 when many became Christians and still do. And it happened in Bangladesh (which was East Pakistan) after its 1971 War of Liberation against the dominant West Pakistanis, where the latter killed many of the Bengalis to try to hold the two sections of the Muslim nation together. In the hospital where our youngest son was born, a man came in and said, "You pray to your God. Ours died in Bangladesh."

The same was evident in Afghanistan. When our family first served there in the early 1970s, there were not many Afghans interested in the Gospel. Then the Soviets invaded Afghanistan in 1979 to support the Afghan communist party. The mujahideen in a Muslim holy war drove them out in 1989, but then their factions began to fight each other in a civil war. The Taliban subsequently took over from 1996 until 2001 to bring in "law and order". During this time many Afghans became refugees in Pakistan where numbers of them became Christians after being disillusioned by the fighting of the mujahideem and the imposition of a strict form of Shariah Law by the Taliban. Many of the new Christians have since returned to Afghanistan.

In Darfur in Western Sudan, a drought in the 1980s led nomadic Arab herdsmen of the north to start invading the African settled farmers' land to the south and the nomadic herdsmen received military help from General al-Bashir of the central government. Thousands were killed. Finally a number of Muslim tribal chiefs came to Christian missionaries and asked for training in the Bible so that they could lead their tribes to peace.

The phenomenal growth of the Kabyle Berber church has certainly been helped by the fact that the Kabyle Berber Muslims of the mountains have felt like second-class citizens to the Arab Muslims of the north. Also it certainly was helped after the civil war between the Islamist rebels and the more liberal Muslim government after the latter canceled the elections in 1991 when it looked like the Islamist Islamic Salvation Front would win the elections. In the ensuing fighting thousands were killed.

David Garrison in a forthcoming book, <u>A Wind in the House of Islam,</u> notes that in the first 13 centuries of Islam there was only one voluntary movement of at least 1,000 Muslim convererts to Christ, the Sadrach Movement of the late 19th and 20th Century in Indonesia. Then there was an influx of 2 million into the church in 1965 when the Communists were defeated and everyone had to join one of five authorized religious communities—Muslims, Protestants, Catholics, Hindus, or Buddists. Between 1980 and 2000 there were eight new movements—Iran (2), Algeria (1), Bangladesh (2), and Central Asia (3). Thus there had been only 10 movements by the end of the 20th Century. But in the first 12 years of this century there have been 64 new movements—in sub-Saharan Africa, the Persian world, the Arab world, Turkistan, South Asia, and Southeast Asia.[37] God has used our Fuller graduates in some of these.

Concurrent with these movements by God, mission personnel have been trying to understand the Muslim World and how God is drawing people to himself. In 1978 a consultation was held in Colorado Springs that looked at the unreached Muslim people groups. With the dearth of converts from Islam at the time, scholars, drawing heavily on church growth principles and anthropology coupled with Scriptures, suggested practices that might be fruitful with Muslims. This resulted in a book

---

[37] D. Garrison, "God Is Doing Something Historic," <u>Mission Frontiers</u> 35 no.4 (Jul-Aug 2013), 6-9.

The Gospel and Islam,[38] and was followed by a series of consultations sponsored by the Muslim Track of the Lausanne Committee for World Evangelization.[39] Meanwhile, Muslims were beginning to follow Christ in greater numbers.

At the beginning of the new millennium Rick Love and other younger leaders covenanted to work together toward planting fellowships of Christ's disciples among every Muslim people group. Initially 13 agencies comprised of 5,800 workers worked together for three to four years to update information of every Muslim people group and to identify fruitful practices that God was blessing. They appreciated the blending of the divine and human in Paul's words "I planted, Apollos watered, but God gave the growth" (I Cor 3:6 NRSV).

Then a consultation was held in Thailand in 2007 for practitioners and mission executives from 56 agencies. The practitioners evaluated the fruitful practice. Some interesting observations surfaced. Forty percent of the church plants were in contexts that had experienced social upheavals or national disasters. A majority of the church plants that gave signs of developing into movements were contextualized to the local culture and were in pre-existing social networks where trust already existed. Use of the heart language was far more effective than the trade language. The moral character of the witnesses was most important. The mission executives then began adopting Muslim people groups that were unengaged with the Gospel. The results are gathered in a volume From Seed to Fruit: Global Trends, Fruitful Practices, and Emerging Issues[40] and the demographic material is updated and circulated every two months. The emerging issues dealing with fruitful practices are on topics such as the factors that influence the identity that Jesus followers choose, factors that facilitate fellowships becoming movements, the oral use of scripture (since 75% of the practitioners worked with peoples preferring oral learning), and empowering indigenous leaders.

---

[38] Ed. D. McCurry, Monrovia, CA: MARC/World Vision Int, 1979.

[39] E.g., Woodberry, ed., Muslims and Christians on the Emmaus Road. Monrovia, CA: MARC/World Vision Resources, 1989.

[40] Ed. Woodberry. Pasadena, CA: William Carey, 2008, rev. 2011.

We started with the image of a cross within a crescent on the flag of the Egyptian Independence Movement of 1919. The earliest known representation of this image is on a 12th Century lamp during the latter Crusades, a previous time of trouble between the Muslim and Christian communities. May God grant that in such a time as this we, like that lamp, might bring the light—Christ's light—into a dark world.

KOREAN UNITY—SEEKING FOR ONE FLAG IN PLACE OF THE TWO

The Christian Pilgrimage in Korea

Joseph Kang, Monte Vista Grove Homes Musings, October 28, 2013

Therefore, since we are justified by faith, we have peace with God through our Lord Jesus Christ, through whom we have obtained access to this grace in which we stand; and we boast in our hope of sharing the glory of God. And not only that, but we also boast in our sufferings, knowing that suffering produces endurance, and endurance produces character, and character produces hope, and hope does not disappoint us, because God's love has been poured into our hearts through the Holy Spirit that has been given to us. (Rom 5:1-5)

INTRODUCTION

In his poetry during the late '60s and 70s, a well-known Korean poet Kim, Ji-ha frequently employed two Korean words: "*han*" (한,恨) and "*tong-gok*" (통곡, 痛哭). *Han* means a grudge from the recess of the heart, a state of groaning under helplessness and deprivation, and *tong-gok* is a lamentation from the depth of heart. Kim explains that *han* and *tong-gok* are at the bottom of Korean people's mind, due to continuous political oppression and economic exploitation throughout their history.[41] A suffering history—this statement may well sum up Korean history. It is the ground of what even today's Korean people

---

[41] Born on February 4, 1941 in Cholla Province, South Korea, Kim studied Korean literature at Seoul National University from 1959. He took part in the 1964 Student Movement activities opposing the military dictatorship, and was arrested, imprisoned and tortured. Graduating from the University in 1966, he was working on movie scripts and theater workshop and published *Five Bandits* between 1968 and 1970, which led to his arrest again. He was imprisoned until December 1980. During his imprisonment he wrote several other poems and a play, *The Gold-Crown Jesus*. Some of them were translated into English by C.S. Kim and Shelly Killen and published by Orbis Books in 1978 with the title, *The Gold Crown Jesus and Other Writings: Kim Chi-Ha.*

stand—a *divided nation under two flags and divided churches* in the midst of explosive economic/religious growth.

And yet, as Viktor Frankl wrote, "If there is meaning in life at all, then there must be a meaning in suffering."[42] In this regards, what Paul wrote in his letter to the first century Roman Christians becomes quite relevant to the Korean people's experience:

"We boast in our hope of sharing the glory of God. And not only that, but we also boast in our sufferings, knowing that suffering produces endurance, and endurance produces character, and character produces hope, and hope does not disappoint us . . ." (Rom 5: 2-4).

It is my privilege to share with you today the history of *han* and *tonggok* among the Korean people. At the same time it is my great joy to share with you the *hope produced by the character* of Korean people as well.

KOREA (Korean: 한국or 조선) is an East Asian territory, located on the Korean Peninsula, and looks like a rabbit. Total area is 85,219 sq mi. (The State of California is 163,696 sq mi.)

Korea is bordered by China to the northwest and Russia to the northeast. It is separated from Japan to the east by the Korea Strait and the Sea of Japan (East Sea). Now it is divided into two separate sovereign states, North and South Korea.

The word, 'Korea' derived from the *Goryeo* period of Korean history, which in turn referred to the ancient kingdom of *Goguryeo*, the first Korean dynasty visited by Persian merchants who referred to *Koryŏ* (Goryeo; 고려) as Korea. *Koryŏ* (Goryeo) is also the name of *Goguryeo*, which changed its name to *Koryŏ* (Goryeo) in the 5th century. Korea is now commonly used in English contexts by both North and South Korea. In the Korean language, Korea as a whole is referred to as *Han-guk* in South Korea, and *Chosŏn* in North Korea. The latter name, also Romanised *Joseon*, is from the *Joseon* Dynasty and the earlier *Gojoseon*. '*The Land of the Morning Calm*' is an English language title for the country loosely derived from the *hanja* characters for *Joseon*.

---

[42]   *Man's Search for Meaning.* Boston: Beacon Press, 2006. p 67.

WHO ARE KOREANS?

1. Once Upon a Time: the Dangun Legend

Gojoseon's founding legend describes *Dangun*,[43] a descendent of heaven, as establishing the kingdom in 2333 BC until the fall in 108 BC. The original capital may have been at the Manchuria-Korea border, but was later moved to what is today Pyongyang, North Korea.

Two socio-anthropological DNAs of Korean people implied by the *Dangun* myth could be pointed out:

a. Feministic feature: In the first part of the story there is no indication whether the two animals were male or female. Yet the bear turned to be a woman who marries the heavenly king. This female bear becomes the mother of *Dangun*. It signifies shyness and introversion, a feministic feature of Korean people. Affection (even irrational, '*jeong*', 정,情) might be another feature of it.

b. Endurance/Perseverance: The bear endures three weeks in the cave eating only the garlic and the mugwort. Tiger couldn't stand, and ran away. Korean people like the bear, throughout their exploitative and oppressive history, demonstrate tremendous ability to endure suffering and hardship.

2. The timeline of Korean history

Prehistory
Gojoseon: Dan-Gun (2333 BC)
Gija Joseon: ?—194 BC
Wiman Joseon: 194 BC-108 BC
Four Commanderies of Han: 108 BC-75 BC

Three Kingdoms (Buddhism introduced in 369AD)
Goguryeo: 37 BC-668 AD
Baekje: 18 BC-660 AD

---

[43] See Appendix I for the legend.

Silla: 57 BC-935 AD

North and South States
Unified Silla: 668-935
Balhae: 698-926

Later Three Kingdoms (892-936)
Hubaekje: 892-936
Taebong: 901-918
Silla:—935

Unitary dynasties period
Goryeo: 918-1392
Joseon: 1392-1910 (Confucianism favored; Christianity introduced)

Colonial Korea (1910-45)

Provisional Government (1919-48)

Division of Korea

North Korea: 1948-present
South Korea: 1948-present

Beginning in the 1870s, Japan began to force Korea out of the Manchu Qing Dynasty's traditional sphere of influence into its own. As a result of the Sino-Japanese War (1894-95), the Qing Dynasty had to give up such a position according to Article 1 of the Treaty of Shimonoseki, which was concluded between China and Japan in 1895. That same year, Empress Myeongseong was assassinated by Japanese agents.

In 1897, the Joseon dynasty proclaimed the Korean Empire (1897-1910), and King Gojong became Emperor Gojong. This brief period saw the partially successful modernization of the military, economy, real property laws, education system, and various industries, influenced by the political encroachment into Korea of Russia, Japan, France, and the United States. In 1910, an already militarily occupied Korea was a forced party to the Japan-Korea Annexation Treaty.

With the surrender of Japan in 1945 the United Nations developed plans for a trusteeship administration, the Soviet Union administering the peninsula north of the 38th parallel and the United States administering the south. The politics of the Cold War resulted in the 1948 establishment of two separate governments, North Korea and South Korea.

WHY TWO FLAGS?

1. Division of Korea with the Two Flags

The aftermath of World War II left Korea separated along the 38th parallel, with the north under Soviet occupation and the south under US occupation supported by other allied states. Consequently, the Democratic People's Republic of Korea, a Soviet-style socialist republic, was established in the north while the Republic of Korea, a Western-style regime, was established in the South. The Korean Peninsula ever since remains divided with the two flags. The Korean Demilitarized Zone being the de facto border between the two states.

 The flag of South Korea or *Taegeukgi* (also spelled Taegukgi) has three parts: a white background; a red and blue *taegeuk* (also known as Taiji and Yinyang) in the center; and four black trigrams, one in each corner of the flag. These trigrams are carried over from the eight trigrams (*Ba gua*), which are of Daoist origin. Taiji, Trigrams and Taoism are parts of the Korean Culture which originated in China.

The white background symbolizes "cleanliness of the people". The *Taegeuk* represents the origin of all things in the universe; holding the two principles of *yin* and *yang* in perfect balance; the former being the negative aspect rendered in blue, and the latter as the positive aspect rendered in red. Together, they represent a continuous movement within infinity, the two merging as one.

The flag was designed by King Gojong or Pak Yeong-hyo in 1882 by the deletion of four of these trigrams, and *Taegeukgi* was adopted as the national flag of Joseon Dynasty on March 6, 1883.

After independence, both North and South Korea adopted versions of the *Taegeukgi*, but North Korea changed its national flag to a more Soviet-inspired design after three years.

The Constituent Assembly of the Republic of Korea (South Korea) adopted the *Taegeukgi* as the national flag on July 12, 1948. After the establishment of the government of the Republic of Korea, "The Rules for the Flag of the Republic of Korea" were first enacted.

 The flag of North Korea is characterized with a red field and blue and white lines at the top and bottom part. There is also a white disk in the middle with a red star in it. The colors red, white and blue are known as the traditional colors of the Korean flag and when North Korea became independent in 1948 and the separated Korea was divided into the two independent states, North Korea retained this color but gave more emphasis to the color red.

The red star in the flag symbolizes the Communist ideals of the state while the white disk is a stylized representation of the *taeguekgi*. The *taeguekgi* was used in the Korean flag upon the country's independence from Japan. Later this design was modified to bear more resemblance to the USSR flag. The overwhelming red stripes found in the North Korean flag represent revolutionary beliefs. The blue stripes signify sovereignty, peace, and friendship. The white stripes represent purity. The North Korean flag was amended on September 8, 1948 to be the National flag of North Korea.

2. Divided Korean Families

In June 1950 North Korea invaded the South, using Soviet tanks and weaponry. During the Korean War (1950-53) more than one million people died and the three years of fighting throughout the nation effectively destroyed most cities. The war ended in an Armistice Agreement at approximately the Military Demarcation Line.

Of the 1.7 million Americans of Korean descent that now reside in the United States (2010 Census), an estimated 100,000 Korean Americans are divided family members, who still have kin living in North Korea.

The vast majority of these divided family members were separated by the start of the Korean War on June 25, 1950 (65-75%, while 25-35%

were separated after liberation right before the Korean War). Millions uprooted their homes in a matter of days (as Seoul was taken in three days) and fled as refugees, to avoid the calamities of war, while others lost all communication with their relations, due to the iron curtain leaving them in complete darkness regarding the whereabouts and well-being of their loved ones who happened to live in the North.

There were fathers and brothers who left their mothers behind, thinking they would be able to return in a few days, only to lose their relatives for a lifetime. Mothers who left their children behind, only to never be able to see them again. Children who became lost in the mad scramble of huge crowds of people flooding the paths to escape.

By 28 June 2001, a mere 11 months after the first round of reunions in August 2000, 12,664 of the 116,460 original applicants for reunion had died. These figures clearly underline the pressing need for a solution to be found to this issue before the first generation of divided families finally disappear from the two Koreas, and the infringement of their fundamental human rights they have endured for so long becomes irreversible.

Clearly the most stressful psychological factor in their predicament is the uncertainty surrounding their loved ones' fates. 83% had no idea of the whereabouts or status of their relatives. Although a small percentage of respondents (3%) said they had no desire to contact family members in the North, 88% said that they would like to contact their relatives. Tensions between the two sides continue to this day, but the political arena is a far more complicated one.

3. Demographics

In *The Final Crucible*, Lee Ballenger, an ex-US Marine sergeant, described the 1st US Marine Division's battles during the final seven months of the Korean War. He wrote his first impression of Korea at that time: "Probably the first thing that every American remembers of his introduction to Korea was the smell—an indescribable mixture of charcoal, garlic, smoke, human waste, unknown food, and the lingering scent of war. It was not pleasant, but, like everything else, one became accustomed to the odor and it was soon forgotten."[44]

Since the 1960s, the South Korean economy has grown enormously and the economic structure was radically transformed.

Forced labor, executions, and concentration camps were responsible for over one million deaths in North Korea from 1948 to 1987; others have estimated 400,000 deaths in concentration camps alone. Estimates based on the most recent North Korean census suggest that 240,000 to 420,000 people died as a result of the 1990s famine and that there were 600,000 to 850,000 unnatural deaths in North Korea from 1993 to 2008.

The combined population of the Koreans is about 73 million (North Korea: 23 million, South Korea: 50 million). Korea is chiefly populated by a highly homogeneous ethnic group, the Koreans, who speak the Korean language. The number of foreigners living in Korea has also steadily increased since the late 20th century, particularly in South Korea, where more than 1 million foreigners reside. It is estimated that only 26,700 of the old Chinese community now remain in South Korea. However, in recent years, immigration from mainland China has increased; 624,994 persons of Chinese nationality have immigrated to South Korea, including 443,566 of ethnic Korean descent. Small communities of ethnic Chinese and Japanese are also found in North Korea.

	South Korea	**North Korea**
Area	38,691 sq mi	46,528 sq mi
Population	50 million	24 million
GDP (PPP)	$1,614 trillion (12th)	$40 billion
Per Capita	$32,272 (26th)	$1,800
GDP (Nominal)	$1,156 trillion (15th)	$12,4 billion
Per Capita	$23,113 (34th)	$506 ($738-July 11, 2013 report)

---

44   *The Final Crucible. U.S. Marines in Korea*, Vol. 2: 1953. Washington, D.C.: Potomac Books, Inc., 2006. P.14-15.

CHRISTIANITY IN KOREA

Confucian tradition has dominated Korean thought, along with contributions by Buddhism, Taoism, and Korean Shamanism. Since the middle of the 20th century, however, Christianity has competed with Buddhism in South Korea, while religious practice has been suppressed in North Korea.

Although a large segment of the population claims to not be affiliated with any organized religion, most South Korean households continue to observe traditional Buddhist and Confucian philosophies that have been integrated into Korean culture.

1. Early Protestant mission[45]

The practice of Christianity in Korea revolves around two of its largest branches, Protestantism and Catholicism, accounting for 8.6 million and 5.1 million members respectively.

The *Joseon* Dynasty saw the new religion as a subversive influence and persecuted its earliest followers in Korea, culminating in the Catholic Persecution of 1866, in which 8,000 Catholics across the country were killed, including 9 French missionaries. The opening of Korea to the outside world in the following years brought religious toleration for the remaining Catholics and also introduced Protestantism.

The Protestant mission carried on three areas of Christian ministry as described in Matthew 9:39, "Then Jesus went about all the cities and villages, **teaching** in their synagogues, **and proclaiming the good news of the kingdom**, and **curing** every disease and every sickness."

The first Presbyterian missionary in Korea, Horace Newton Allen, arrived in 1884 and remained in Korea until 1890, by which time he had been joined by many others.

---

[45] Description of the early American missionaries is based on Min, Kyung Bae, *History of the Korean Church*, (KCLS, 1968).

Allen was first appointed on a mission to China by the Board of Foreign Missions of the Presbyterian Church and a year later he was sent to work at the United States Legation to Korea as physician.

Arrived with his family on September 20, 1884, he was involved in the aftermath of *Gapsinjeongbyeon*, during which a royal relative Min Young Ik was stabbed and injured. Under his modern medical treatment unknown to Korea at the time, Min Young Ik recovered in three months. Consequently, this initiated for Allen a close connection with Gojong, and demonstrated the benefit of western medicine to the Korean public. With this turn of events Allen was able to establish *Gwanghyewon* (House of Extended Grace) under royal finance and support in Seoul. Gwanghyewon was the first modern medical facility in Korea. The Gwanghyewon was soon renamed by Gojong to *Che Chung Won* (the House of Civilized Virtue) and evolved to become the current Severance Hospital and Yonsei University College of Medicine in Seoul, Korea. He was instrumental to lift the nation's anti-Christianity policy to allow the influx of missionaries to evangelize, build schools and other western hospitals in the Hermit Kingdom.

Horace Underwood, born in London and migrated to United States at the age of 12, and graduated from the New Brunswick Theological Seminary in New Brunswick, New Jersey, arrived in Korea as a missionary, and taught physics and chemistry at *Gwanghyewon*. Underwood worked with Henry G. Appenzeller, William B. Scranton, James Scarth Gale, and William D. Reynolds on the Korean Bible. Translation of the New Testament was completed in 1900, and Old Testament in 1910. In 1900, Underwood and James S. Gale established the Seoul YMCA and in 1915 Underwood became the president of the *Joseon* Christian College, the predecessor of Yonsei University. He wrote several books on Korea, including *The Call of Korea*.

Underwood's older brother, John T. Underwood, was a typewriter entrepreneur based in New York who helped finance Horace Grant's missionary endeavors.

Underwood's physical legacy is visible in various Christian educational institutes in Seoul. There is a statue of him in the center of the Yonsei

University campus, and the Underwood Activity Center of Seoul Foreign School is dedicated to his grandson, Richard F. Underwood. Underwood's descendants have served to develop Korean society, religion, politics and education for over one hundred years. His son Horace Horton Underwood (1890-1951) continued the tradition of education and worked at Yonhi University, another predecessor of Yonsei University.

Henry Gerhard Appenzeller (February 6, 1858-June 11, 1902) was a Methodist missionary. Appenzeller arrived in Korea on April 5, 1885, an Easter Sunday morning, with his wife Ella Appenzeller. During that period, Seoul was in political struggle. Missionaries could not set up a church, nor preach in the public. Evangelism had to be done secretly. Appenzeller focused on preparing missionary residence in the first two years.

Appenzeller was the founder of a boy school—*Baichai Hakdang* in Korea in 1887. He spread the Gospel, introduced Western culture, and trained the students into Methodist. He was one of the founders of the first Korean Methodist Church in Seoul, *Jong Dong*. He served in the *Jong Dong* as a pastor in 1887 until his death in 1902. In 1886, Appenzeller was on the Board of Bible Translators with the other Methodist, Presbyterian missionaries and other Korean translator. He helped to translate the bible into Korea.

In 1902, at the age of 44, Appenzeller drowned while journeying to a southern port city, Mokpo, to attend a meeting for the Bible translation. He was later buried at the *Yanghwajin* Foreigners' Cemetery, the grave site of over 300 foreigners including over 80 missionaries from many denominations including those sent by the United Methodist Church, and its predecessor denominations in the late 19th and early 20th centuries.

2. Church Growth—"Explosiveness of Korean religiosity"

The growth of the Christian church in Korea was gradual until 1945 when about 2% were Christian. A rapid growth of Christianity ensued. "The growth of Korean Protestantism in the past century and a quarter has been extraordinary by any measure. Korean churches experienced rapid numerical growth, in particular from the 1960s through the 1980s. In 1960 the Protestant population was 623,000, and by 1985 it had grown over tenfold to 6,489,000."[46] As of 1991, 54% of the South Korean population identified themselves as religious. Of these 51% were Buddhists, 34% (8.0 million) were Protestants, and 11% (2.5 million) were Catholics. The Catholic Church has increased its membership by 70% in the last ten years. Anglicanism in Korea has also experienced significant growth in the recent decades. Protestantism has been a dynamic force, providing a dynamic standard against which Catholics and Buddhists have been forced to compete. It was the inspiration for numerous sects, such as the Unification Church, founded in 1954 by Sun Myung Moon.

There are numerous mega churches in Korea, whose membership counts more than 100,000. Two of them are to be Youngnak Presbyterian Church and Yoido Full Gospel Church.

Rev. Han Kyung-chik, a Princeton Theological Seminary graduate, and 26 other North Korean Christians fleeing the communist takeover of North Korea founded Youngnak Presbyterian church in Seoul in December 1945.

Today, the church has a congregation of more than 100,000, making it possibly the largest Presbyterian Church in the world. In part thanks to his church's unprecedented growth, Rev. Han won the Templeton Prize, the "Nobel Prize of religion," in 1992.

The Youngnak Presbyterian Church complex is like a Presbyterian city, complete with an 8-story "50th Anniversary Commemorative Hall" capable of holding 10,000. The original church built in 1945 was too small to handle Rev. Han's rapidly growing flock, so in June 1947 a large tent was set up in which to hold services. In March 1949, work began on a new sanctuary befitting the church. A little over a year later, the church was complete. On June 4, 1950, the first service was held in the new church . . . just a couple of weeks before the outbreak of the Korean War.

---

[46] Park, Joon-Sik, "Korean Protestant Christianity: A Missiological Reflection," *International Bulletin of Missionary Research*, 2012

Yoido Full Gospel Church was founded by David Yong-gi Cho in 1973. Theologically in the same line with Robert Shuler's "theology of positive thinking" the Cho's leadership for this church has drawn a membership of 450,000, making it the largest independent church in the world. The Cho has recently retired and 526 ministers are currently working with his successor, Young-hoo Lee.

Se-Woong Koo, a lecturer, Department of Religious Studies, Stanford University, writes "No one has been able to satisfyingly explain the explosiveness of Korean religiosity, but one thing is certain: religions have been an inseparable aspect of Korean life since the beginning and given the present circumstance it does not look as though they will wither away anytime soon. The complexity of Korea's religious dimension is a fascinating, and ongoing, object of study for many scholars."[47]

3.   Factors of Korean Protestant Growth

A visit to Korea in 1890 by John L. Nevius, long-time missionary to China turned out to be missiologically critical, for this was a time when the missionaries were still feeling their way toward an over-all strategy for the evangelization of Korea. The so-called Nevius Plan stressed the crucial importance of native leadership for church growth, and became the universally accepted policy of Protestant mission in Korea spurring the Korean church to be independent and self-supporting.

Translation of the Bible into the Korean language, considered to be the women's language, was very significant factor for spreading the Christian faith among the lower sector of the country as well.

Several other factors might help explain the rapid growth of the Korean Protestant Church.[48]

Historical and geopolitical factors. The historical and geopolitical situations in and around Korea encouraged Koreans to accept

---

[47]   "Religions of Korea Yesterday and Today," *Spice Digest*. Fall, 2010.

[48]   I owe this part to the Koo's article.

Christianity more readily than in other Asian countries. Korea became forcibly annexed by Japan in 1910, and this tragic loss of independence decisively shaped both the nature of Korean nationalism and the life of the Korean church. By the end of the nineteenth century, the majority of Asian nations had become subjugated by Western powers and turned anti-Western; in Korea, however, the nationalism was anti-Japanese. Koreans welcomed Christianity as a viable channel for expressing its nationalistic sentiment against the Japanese. The early growth of Korean Christianity thus became inseparably intertwined with Korean nationalism. The nationwide March First Korean Independence Movement of 1919 serves as a telling illustration of this unique partnership. Of the original thirty-three signatories of the Declaration of Independence, remarkably fifteen were Christians, even though Christians at that time represented only I percent of the population.

Religious factors. Like most Asian countries, over the course of its history Korea has been deeply suffused with diverse religious traditions. The religious tradition of Korea had in a substantial way such congenial elements as the monotheistic concept of God, longing for salvation, messianic hope, and eternal life beyond this worldly life, all of which were conducive to the acceptance of Christianity. In other words, some affinity between traditional Korean religions and Christianity made it easier for Koreans to adopt the Christian faith.

It might be underlined, therefore, that Christian conversions in Korea did not necessarily involve radically disowning formerly held beliefs, in particular those of shamanism. As the oldest religion in Korea, shamanism had taken deep root in the religious beliefs and the worldview of the Korean people. Because of shamanism's enduring and permeating influence, it was typical as well as inevitable for religions later introduced to Korea to assimilate certain of shamanism's beliefs and practices—in particular, its predominant focus on this-worldly and materialistic aspects of life. Christianity was not an exception. It could be safely stated that the phenomenal growth of Korean Christianity in part depended on mitigating possible conflicts between Christian faith and traditional religious values.

Economic factors. From the 1960s through the '80s South Korea has achieved extraordinary economic growth, rebuilding itself from the rubble of war and rapidly becoming an industrialized and urbanized country. In 1990, in a little over a generation from the devastating Korean War, its economy became the fifteenth largest in the world. This swift transition from a rural-agricultural to an urban-industrial society resulted in a mass migration of rural villagers to urban areas, causing a widespread sense of intense dislocation and disorientation. Social instability was inevitable, as well as a steady erosion of long-held values and norms, including the breakdown of the traditional extended family. A deep sense of alienation and up-rootedness spread throughout the country.

It should be noted that the period of the most explosive growth of the Korean church coincided with that of Korea's rapid industrialization, and that the numerical increase of the church mostly occurred in urban areas. Seeking to alleviate their enormous physical and emotional dislocation and alienation, and searching for an alternative community to the close-knit rural social networks, many Koreans turned to churches. The churches in Korea were, however, not merely a passive receptor of newcomers; they actively helped sustain the moral and spiritual values of the nation in the midst of the country's rapid economic transition.

In recent years, however, Protestantism has seen a decline in South Korea due to scandals involving church leadership and conflict among various denominations, as well as negative opinions regarding missionary work by the churches as being too aggressive among the general South Korean public. As a result, a growing number of South Korean Protestants is converting to Buddhism or Catholicism.

Sociological and cultural factors. Confucianism has been an integral part of Korean society and culture since the fifth century. The *Joseon* Dynasty (1392-1910) created the most Confucian society in East Asia, even more fully than in China. From the fifteenth century onward, Confucianism penetrated all facets of the society, regulating family life, culture, and politics. Yet it carried certain values that could readily resonate with or complement those of Christianity. For instance, the early missionaries' pioneering work in modern education was in tune with Confucianism's profound reverence for learning, and the missionaries' strict moral teaching was seen as consistent with the austere moral code of Neo-Confucianism.

Another element of Christianity attractive to Confucians was its stress on filial piety, which was one of the five wheels of relationship[49] considered by Confucius to be the centerpiece of a harmonious society. It would not be an overstatement to say that, in a very real sense, Protestant Christianity was built on the foundation laid by the moral concerns of Neo-Confucianism.

The initial complementarity between Korean Confucianism and Christianity provided a favorable setting for the rapid growth of the Korean church. Eventually, however, Confucianism came to have a negative influence on the development and maturation of Korean Christianity.

The influence of the Christian church on education has been decisive as Churches started 293 schools and 40 universities including 3 of the top 5 academic institutions. Protestantism is seen as the religion of the middle class, youth, intellectuals, and urbanites, and has been central to South Korea's pursuit of modernity and emulation of the United States.

4. Theological/Mission Challenges of Korean Christian Church

   a. From theology of prosperity to socio/economic justice

Since the 1960s, the focus of the Korean Protestant church has been rather exclusively growth-oriented. I would say that its operating evangelical/theological framework is still that of growth, although church membership has been declining remarkably since the late '90.

---

[49] Confucianism follows the Five Constant Relationships: Parent and Child, Husband and Wife, Older Sibling and Younger Sibling, Older Friend and Younger Friend, and Ruler and Subject. The goal of individuals in Neo-Confucianism is to go beyond the material world, and to reach union with the Supreme Ultimate.

Korean churches appear to direct most of its attention to finding ways to reverse it.

An exception has been *minjung* theology, which grew out of the particular experience of South Korean people in their political and socio-economic struggles for justice in the '70s and '80s. It affirms Korean culture and history as the context for a proper Korean theology, regarding the biblical stories and the social biographies of the suffering *minjung* (민중, 民衆, lit., "the mass of the people") as the two primary reference points. Minjung theology arose in protest against the overall apolitical stance of Korean evangelicalism and its indifference to systemic injustices; it has challenged Korean Christianity to be more integral and prophetic in its theology and practice of mission and to be on the side of the disenfranchised *minjung.*

Quite simply, Korean Protestants need to make a radical change in their ecclesiology and theology. They need to listen humbly to the biblical teaching on unity and reconciliation as the proper focus and ethos of all their mission and evangelism.

Korean churches have been rather exclusively preoccupied with personal salvation and piety, ignoring the call of the Gospel to social and cultural transformation. Korean Christians' understanding of discipleship needs to be broadened and deepened so as to include seeking justice as well as caring for the poor, the excluded, and the victimized. They now need to heed to the central importance of the Christian community as a new humanity or as a new kind of social reality. The mission of the church is first and foremost to be and remain a faithful community of faith with a new and distinctive identity and life. Working for new humanity and mission cannot be separated, and the life of the church should not invalidate its witness.[50] Evangelism and mission are practicable and feasible only when there is

---

[50] In this sense Christology of the Son of Human Being needs to be renewed. See, Kang, Joseph, *Doing Theology Through Stories. A Study of the Synoptic Gospel Stories for Renewal of Preaching in the Korean Church.* SFTS STD Dissertation. 1981. Esp. Chapter II and V.

a community whose life reflects differences from the rest of the world, in particular with regard to power, Mammon, and violence.

b. Church in Partnership of Ministry for Healing, Peace and Reunification

The Gospel as a message of peace is crucially pertinent to Korean churches, for participating in national reunification remains an important part of their mission. A small segment of the Korean church has actively engaged in the reunification movement, in particular since the 1980s. Yet the general sentiment among Korean Christians settles for a strong anti-Communist position, which has kept them from engaging reunification issues from a biblically informed perspective of reconciliation, and from moving beyond their evangelistic interest and humanitarian concern toward undertaking peacemaking initiatives. Korean Christianity needs to be reminded afresh that witness to peace is something very central to the Gospel, and always the most important part of the Gospel. It is crucial for the Korean church to construct a *theology of reconciliation* based upon the peace message of the Gospel, for without forgiveness of the past history between the North and the South, genuine reunification is not likely.[51]

Mission to North Korea could well be a test case for the integrity of the Korean missionary movement. It definitely would be a cross-cultural mission, for North and South Korea have lived in two different ideological and political systems for more than six decades. Given the economic superiority of the South, it is critically important that missionaries welcome North Koreans with both respect and care. Mission and evangelism must be carried out with sensitivity to the fragility of North Koreans, resulting particularly from the heavy economic dependence on the South that can be expected of North Koreans. For South Koreans to welcome and accept North Korean

---

[51] For the political science perspective, see, Kwak, Tae-Hwan & Joo, Seung-Ho, *Peace Regime Building on the Korean Peninsula and Northwest Asian Security Cooperation*. Burlington:Ashgate Pub. Co , 2010; and Han, Sang-Jin, ed., *Divided Nations and Transitional Justice: What Germany, Japan and South Korea Can Teach the World*. Paradigm Publishers, 2010.

defectors would be a very important precedent for the Korean church's mission of reconciliation toward North Korea.

It is also pivotal for Korean missionaries to extend partnership and the spirit of 'working together' to one another, and thus to overcome competitiveness and rivalry. In light of the temptation to impose denominational patterns and structures on other churches, it is crucial that missionaries guard themselves from creating or perpetuating on the mission field the divisions experienced in Korean Protestantism. Partnership in mission through the practice of ecumenical coordination is crucially important, in particular in the future mission to North Korea. The North Korean Church Reconstruction Council, formed in 1995 by the Korean National Council of Churches (KNCC), presented a three-stage plan for rebuilding the churches in North Korea: first, to form a single channel of evangelization to prevent missionary competition; second, to build a single Christian denomination without transplanting the schisms and splits of the South to the North; and, third, ultimately to enable churches in North Korea to be independent and self-reliant without the domination of South Korean churches. For such a plan to succeed, true ecumenical unity among the churches in South Korea should first be embodied through the practice of welcoming and showing tolerance to each other.

CONCLUSION

The Christian faith was introduced from the West to Korea and has been the crucial engine of personal/social transformation. Its seed was sown in a fertile soil and has been growing in an immeasurable scale. Despite some negative theological/missiological elements, there is no doubt that the Korean Church would bear abundant fruits in its prophetic and priestly ministry as long as it works for socio-economic justice and the reconciliation/reunification between the North and the South.

It is not a mere coincidence that the 10th Assembly of the World Council of Churches is going to be held in Busan, the farther Southern port city of Korea from October 30 until November 8, 2013. With a population of more than 4 million people, Busan is the second largest city in South Korea. The Assembly will be the first WCC assembly taking place in Northeast Asia and the broader Asian context will significantly shape the gathering. The theme of the Assembly, *"God of Life, lead us to Justice and Peace"* is quite appropriate not only for the world churches but also for the Korean churches in its particular situation—the homogenous people of one same language and cultural heritage, yet divided by the six decade old ideology and hatred. It is our ardent prayer that one flag would be raised again in place of the two that symbolizes such division and hatred.

The Korean concept of *madang* will serve to root the assembly in the host context and help to give it shape and meaning. *Madang* is the traditional Korean "courtyard" connecting different parts of a house; a space for discussion, deliberation, celebration and fellowship; a traditional center of family and community life. The WCC assembly will be prepared in a spirit of *madang*, inviting participants into a common space of discussion and celebration.

I want to close this presentation with reading the passage from Ephesians 2:11-22:

So then, remember that at one time you Gentiles by birth, called 'the un-circumcision' by those who are called 'the circumcision'—a physical circumcision made in the flesh by human hands—remember that you were at that time without Christ, being aliens from the commonwealth of Israel, and strangers to the covenants of promise, having no hope and without God in the world.

But now in Christ Jesus you who once were far off have been brought near by the blood of Christ. For he is our peace; in his flesh he has made both groups into one and has broken down the dividing wall, that is, the hostility between us.

He has abolished the law with its commandments and ordinances, so that he might create in himself one new humanity in place of the two, thus making peace, and might reconcile both groups to God in one body through the cross, thus putting to death that hostility through it.

So he came and proclaimed peace to you who were far off and peace to those who were near; for through him both of us have access in one Spirit to the Father.

So then you are no longer strangers and aliens, but you are citizens with the saints and also members of the household of God, built upon the foundation of the apostles and prophets, with Christ Jesus himself as the cornerstone.

In him the whole structure is joined together and grows into a holy temple in the Lord; in whom you also are built together spiritually into a dwelling-place for God.

RESOURCES:

Adams, Daniel J., *Korean Theology in Historical Perspective*. Delhi: ISPCK, 2012.

Ballenger, Lee. *U.S. Marines in Korea*, Vol. 1: 1952. Washington, D.C. : Brassey's. 2000; *The Final Crucible. U.S. Marines in Korea*, Vol. 2: 1953. Washington, D.C.: Potomac Books, Inc. 2001.

Han, Sang-Jin, ed., *Divided Nations and Transitional Justice: What Germany, Japan and South Korea Can Teach the World*. Paradigm Publishers, 2010.

Kang, Joseph, *"Doing Theology" Through Stories: A Study of the Synoptic Gospel Stories for Renewal of Preaching in the Korean Church*, SFTS STD Dissertation, 1981.

Kim, C.S. and Killen, Shelly, *The Gold Crown Jesus and Other Writings: Kim Chi-Ha*, Orbis Books, 1978.

Koo, Se-Woong, "Religions of Korea Yesterday and Today," *Spice Digest*, Fall, 2010.

Kwak, Tae-Hwan & Joo, Seung-Ho, ed., *Peace Regime Building on the Korean Peninsula and Northwest Asian Security Cooperation*. Burlington: Ashgate Pub. Co., 2010.

Lederach, John P., *Building Peace: Sustainable Reconciliation in Divided Societies*. Washington, D.C.: US Institute of Peace, 1997 3rd. KT: 평화는 어떻게 만들어지는가.

Min, Kyung-Bae, *A Collection of Works on the History of Korea* (Korean). (Yonsei Uni. Press, 1994).

Moffett, Samuel Hugh, *The Christians of Korea*. New York: Friendship Press, 1962.

Moon, Steve Sang-Cheol, "Missions from Korea 2013: Micro-trends and Finance", *International Bulletin of Missionary Research.*2013.

Park, Joon-Sik, "Korean Protestant Christianity: A Missiological Reflection", *International Bulletin of Missionary Research*, 2012.

Appendix I: **The Legend of Dan-Gun**

Dan-gun Wang-geom (단군왕검, 檀君王儉), or *Dan-gun*(단군, 檀君), was the legendary founder of *Gojoseon*, the first Korean kingdom, around present-day Liaoning, Manchuria, and the Korean Peninsula. He is said to be the "grandson of heaven", and to have founded the kingdom in 2333 BC. The earliest recorded version of the *Dan-gun* legend appears in the 13th century *Samguk Yusa*, which cites China's Book of Wei and Korea's lost historical record *Gogi* (古記).

Dan-gun's ancestry legend begins with his grandfather *Hwan-in* (환인; 桓因), the "Lord of Heaven". *Hwan-in* had a son, *Hwan-ung*, who yearned to live on the earth among the valleys and the mountains. *Hwan-in* permitted *Hwan-ung* and 3,000 followers to descend onto *Baekdu* Mountain, where *Hwan-ung* founded *Sinsi* (신시; 神市, "City of God"). Along with his ministers of clouds, rain, and wind, he instituted laws and moral codes and taught humans various arts, medicine, and agriculture. Legend attributes the development of acupuncture and moxibustion to *Dan-gun*.

A tiger and a bear prayed to *Hwan-ung* that they might become human. Upon hearing their prayers, *Hwan-ung* gave them 20 cloves of garlic and a bundle of mugwort, ordering them to eat only this sacred food and remain out of the sunlight for 100 days. The tiger gave up after about twenty days and left the cave. However, the bear remained and was transformed into a woman. The bear and the tiger are said to represent two tribes that sought the favor of the heavenly prince.

The bear-woman (*Ung-nyeo*; 웅녀; 熊女) was grateful and made offerings to *Hwan-ung*. However, she lacked a husband, and soon became sad and prayed beneath a "*Sindansu*" (신단수; 神檀樹, "Divine Betula") tree to be blessed with a child. *Hwan-ung*, moved by her prayers, took her for his wife and soon she gave birth to a son, who was named *Dan-gun Wang-geom*.

Dan-gun ascended to the throne, built the walled city of *Asadal*, situated near Pyongyang (the location is disputed) and called the kingdom *Joseon*—referred to today as "Old/Ancient Joseon" (Korean: "*Gojoseon*") so as not to be confused with the *Joseon* kingdom which occurred much later. He then moved his capital to *Asadal* on Mount *Baegak* (or Mount *Gunghol*).

ACKNOWLEDGMENTS

One of the pleasures of living at The Grove is the friendship shared with our six writers. Each of them has a unique perspective on both faith and culture, and it has been an honor to work with them on this book. The project would not have been possible without the enthusiastic support of Deborah Herbert, Executive Director of Monte Vista Grove Homes. Her predecessor as Executive Director, Helen Baatz, was instrumental in helping me initiate our lecture series, Monte Vista Musings, which is the basis for each chapter.

Meagan McClellan, Events Coordinator and Philanthropy Assistant for The Grove, coordinated the lecture series with grace and a catching smile, and she created the cover design for our book. Resident Margy Wentz has been a crucial helper, carefully proofing and editing the copy. Bill Craig and I are co-chairs of the Convocation Committee at The Grove, and this group has been a good sounding board as we have planned both the Musings lecture series and the book. Behind the scenes, my wife Marilyn has provided wise counsel and encouragement throughout the process. Finally, I thank all the residents of Monte Vista Grove for their support of our lecture series, and for the ongoing conversations at the juncture of faith and our 21st century culture.

ABOUT THE AUTHORS

F. Dale Bruner is the Wasson Emeritus Professor of Theology, Whitworth University, and the author of commentaries on the Gospels of Matthew, John, and the Holy Spirit in the Book of Acts ("A Theology of the Holy Spirit"). He now teaches the Adult Sunday School Class at the First Presbyterian Church of Hollywood.

Gary Demarest brings 65 years of active ministry to his Musings . . . 10 years in youth ministry . . . 35 years a Pastor . . . 5 years Presbyterian General Assembly Evangelism Staff . . . global ministries in Africa and Central America . . . 6 Interim pastorates . . . currently serving the La Verne Heights Presbyterian Church as Supply Pastor.

Born in South Korea, **Joseph Kang** earned a ThM degree from Hankuk Theological Seminary in Seoul and a STD degree from San Francisco Theological Seminary. After serving two Korean-American congregations he followed his passion for teaching biblical studies at theological seminaries in Malawi and Russia.

Jane Atkins Vásquez studied at Washington University in St. Louis, the University of Madrid and the University of New Mexico. She is a Presbyterian Ruling Elder and heads the Program for Hispanic Lay Leader Training (PALL) in the Synod of Southern California and Hawaii. She teaches and writes about Hispanic Christian history.

Franklin Woo taught in Hong Kong and directed the China Program, National Council of Churches in the U.S.A. From relations between churches in HK, China, and America, he is committed to building inclusivity in a multipolar world. His forte is intercultural interaction, with respect leading to understanding and mutual transformation.

J. Dudley Woodberry is Dean Emeritus and Senior Professor of Islamic Studies in the School of Intercultural Studies at Fuller Theological Seminary. He previously served on the staff of the Christian Study Centre in Rawalpindi, Pakistan, and as the pastor of the churches in Kabul, Afghanistan, and Riyadh, Saudi Arabia.

CPSIA information can be obtained at www.ICGtesting.com
Printed in the USA
LVOW13s0837311213

367458LV00003B/10/P